Inequalities in the]

Inequalities in the Early Years examines poverty's effects on children and provides workable solutions for decreasing childhood inequalities through the formal education process. This powerful edited collection explores early childhood inequalities across ten disciplines: earth sciences and geography, life sciences, physical sciences, technology, mathematics, history, society and social institutions, business and economy, the arts, and sports and recreation, following Kipfer's delineation of broad subject areas of knowledge. The volume reaches beyond the domain of education to include multiple perspectives from scholars in the aforementioned disciplines.

Bonnie Johnson is Professor of Education at St. John's University, New York City.

Yvonne Pratt-Johnson is Professor of Education at St. John's University, New York City.

Inequalities in the Early Years

Edited by Bonnie Johnson and
Yvonne Pratt-Johnson

Routledge
Taylor & Francis Group

NEW YORK AND LONDON

First published 2018
by Routledge
711 Third Avenue, New York, NY 10017

and by Routledge
2 Park Square, Milton Park, Abingdon, Oxon, OX14 4RN

Routledge is an imprint of the Taylor & Francis Group, an informa business

© 2018 Taylor & Francis

The right of Bonnie Johnson and Yvonne Pratt-Johnson to be
identified as the authors of the editorial material, and of the authors
for their individual chapters, has been asserted in accordance with
sections 77 and 78 of the Copyright, Designs and Patents Act 1988.

Library of Congress Cataloging-in-Publication Data
A catalog record for this title has been requested

ISBN: 978-1-138-08602-9 (hbk)
ISBN: 978-1-138-08603-6 (pbk)
ISBN: 978-1-315-11115-5 (ebk)

Typeset in Bembo
by Swales & Willis Ltd, Exeter, Devon, UK

Printed and bound by CPI Group (UK) Ltd, Croydon, CR0 4YY

In loving memory of Dale D. Johnson
Humanitarian, Scholar

and

To Raphael N. Johnson for his unwavering love, constant
encouragement, and endless support

Contents

Foreword

When Professors Bonnie Johnson and Yvonne Pratt-Johnson asked me if I would be willing to write the Foreword to this book, Inequalities in the Early Years, written by St. John's administrators and faculty, I immediately felt an affinity to the topic because as President of St. John's University, I am keenly aware of the effects of income inequality on the ability of students to obtain a college degree. While my academic and administrative experience has been in higher education and not in early education, this book has shown me the gravity and complexity of the effects of poverty on a child's well-being and the limitations that poverty imposes on their ability to learn and acquire a strong academic foundation at an early age.

In my role as a president focused on the Catholic and Vincentian mission of providing access to a quality college education, especially for those who might otherwise not be able to afford it, and ensuring student success by helping them to graduate from college, I have seen the challenges that college-age students from low-income families have to overcome in order to succeed. If young children are held back by poverty from making progress during their early years in school, their chances of completing high school, much less going to college, are very slim. It is clear that if we are to improve the level of educational attainment in our citizenry, those efforts have to start in the early years of a child's existence.

The intent of this book is to examine the effects of early childhood inequalities across several subject areas, namely: technology, mathematics, literacy, life sciences, business marketing, society and social institutions, history, the arts, sports and recreation, physical sciences, and geography. The multidisciplinary analyses provided by the chapter authors include case-specific perspectives of scholars from different disciplines on poverty's effects on children and possible policy recommendations for lessening these inequalities.

The book covers issues as basic as insufficient food and clothing, inadequate shelter or homelessness, lack of health care, and limited adult supervision because parents are working multiple minimum-wage jobs, serving time in prison, or suffering from addiction. The book also deals with broader issues of neighborhood violence, underfunded schools, using standardized tests for all children without regard to their socio-economic background, and the physical, psychological, social, and economic impact of poverty on child development. The authors explain in detail how the effects of poverty permeate every aspect of a child's life and influences his/her self-image and world view.

The first chapter, entitled "Technology: Factors behind the Digital Divide," discusses the early childhood education challenge of having limited resources to access technology for learning since economically poor children and their families must prioritize their basic need for food, clothing, and shelter, which they can barely meet. The second chapter, entitled "Mathematics and Measurements: Young Children Count," explains the importance of investing in young children's future in mathematics and how the uniform nature of standardized tests put poor children at a much greater disadvantage because these standards do not account for their lack of resources. The third chapter, entitled "Literacy: Poverty, Literacy, and the American Dream," raises the question: why do many poor young children fail to become readers in the primary schools of America and what are the causes of illiteracy? The author examines what the government has done to help, and discusses best practices of teaching reading to children in poor and urban settings.

The fourth chapter, entitled "Physical Sciences: Pediatric Medical Conditions Associated with Poverty," details the impact of poverty on pediatric medical conditions and how teachers must work closely with health care providers to overcome these health challenges. The fifth chapter, entitled "Business and Economics: The Transformative Potential of Marketing to Fight Child Poverty," highlights the role of transformative consumer research in poverty alleviation and provides two case studies of marketplace solutions. The sixth chapter, entitled "Society and Social Institutions: The Racial, Spatial, and Intergenerational Contours of Food Inequality in America," addresses the serious consequences of food insecurity in early childhood and the importance of giving people the resources to create thriving food economies in their neighborhoods.

The seventh chapter, entitled "History: The Evolution of Juvenile Justice," describes the history of the juvenile justice system and its relationship with the vicious cycle of poverty. The eighth chapter, entitled "The Arts: Arts Education and Makerspaces," explains why the combined approach of arts education and the maker movement is critical in promoting discovery learning and increasing opportunities for arts education in low-income areas. The ninth chapter, entitled "Sports and Recreation: Inequalities for Young Children with Regards to Sports and Physical Activity," discusses the impact of poverty on access to athletic and sporting activities and proposes a set of recommendations to address the lack of access.

The tenth chapter, entitled "Life Sciences: Reaching for the Stars from the Start," highlights the role of disciplinary knowledge in the sciences to foster young children's scientific observation skills while acknowledging that obtaining the resources to teach these skills can be challenging for underfunded schools. The eleventh chapter, entitled "Earth Sciences and Geography: How Geographic Settings Contribute to Child Poverty with Implications for Child Citizenship Development," examines the similarities of the impact of poverty on children in the United States, Ireland, and Nigeria. The author concludes that no matter how or where the children experience poverty, its impact can be consequential, particularly in their development as citizens.

President Obama has said that the dream of upward economic mobility is breaking down and the growing income inequality "is a defining challenge of our time." I believe those of us in education have a distinct opportunity to help alleviate income inequality and promote economic and social mobility. In order to reduce income inequality, serious efforts must be made to improve opportunities for those who are disadvantaged so they can avail themselves of adequate primary and secondary-level education that will qualify them to go to college. If those who are poor and socially disadvantaged are effectively shut out from getting the education they need in order to improve their lives, then income inequality will continue to grow and that is not good for society as a whole.

I am very proud to be part of this much-needed book since it reflects the values of our Catholic and Vincentian mission. It illustrates that as an academic community, St. John's is an institution that works together across disciplines to help those most in need by giving voice to members of society who are often forgotten and recommending solutions to eradicate social injustice and inequalities. Many readers of this book are educators and policy makers who have dedicated their careers to helping the younger generation. We are all given this unique opportunity to transform the lives of our students and shape the future generation. This book reminds us that while we face serious challenges, we must not lose sight of the role and importance of education in reducing income inequality and promoting economic and social mobility.

Conrado "Bobby" Gempesaw
President, St. John's University,
New York City

Preface

Autumn Tooms Cyprès, Associate Dean for Research for Graduate Studies, The School of Education, St. John's University

Although the term *social justice* is used commonly in global, national, and everyday discourses, its definition remains unclear and a point of argument for educators and policy makers. Scholars (e.g., Shields, Bogotch, & Tooms, 2007; Tooms & Boske, 2010) have long investigated questions such as "What does social justice mean in terms of educational policy or leadership?" and "What does social justice mean in terms of daily action?" More specifically, scholars of leadership in education have traced the origins of *social justice* to the Catholic Intellectual Traditions (Shoho, Merchant, & Lugg, 2005). Among these traditions are the *Corporal Works of Mercy* that include feeding the hungry, giving drink to the thirsty, visiting the sick, and giving shelter to the homeless. Addressing issues of poverty as a necessary responsibility of humanity is a clear motif woven in these merciful acts. Like many of my colleagues at St. John's University (an institution built to serve immigrants and the poor), the intersections of social justice and education rest in daily acts of teaching, service, and scholarship. This scholarly effort examines a frontier not often deconstructed in education: the intersections of poverty and early childhood education.

The book opens with Johnson and Pratt-Johnson's consideration of factors contributing to the digital divide and uses observances and lessons from everyday life in the classroom. From there, readers will find chapter explorations ranging from wide-sweeping "Up There" socio-political topics to subjects grounded in the lived experiences of children in poverty. This volume is written for scholars as well as for educators; therefore, insights specific to many classroom disciplines (i.e., literacy, math, history, the arts, geography, technology, and science) are offered.

Societal interrogations, such as Cadet, Rubin, and Ball's look at how marketing practices can transform understandings of poverty (Chapter 5), Rodriguez's interrogation of race and food inequality (Chapter 6), and McClure's discussion of how poverty is defined through a global and geographic lens (Chapter 11), are nested poignantly with the deconstructed challenges in the classroom that educators, scholars, and policy makers might not have considered. For example, Broderick (Chapter 7) examines how the history/evolution of the American juvenile justice system contributed to a reflexive mechanism of poverty. Schamroth Abrams (Chapter 8) describes how arts education and the maker movement can not only raise social consciousness but also empower learners to be change agents. Chase (Chapter 9) deftly deconstructs how opportunity and type of physical activity differ for children of poverty along with prescriptives to challenge the status quo. Stehling and Mangione (Chapter 4) explain the challenges of asthma in young children in terms of diagnosis, treatment, and access to medication. Morabito (Chapter 10) and Ness (Chapter 2) offer separate but harmonizing discussions considering children's curiosity and the ways in which words are used to inspire or marginalize. Morabito frames the inquiry with explorations in life science, and Ness takes a peek through the lens of mathematics. Sampson (Chapter 3) adds to the conversation with a combination of personal narrative and pedagogy to share two instructional models meant to foster literacy growth.

Buckle up, gentle reader; this book is a turbulent ride of insights that many of us will not have considered simply because of our own privilege. It is a necessary tone poem to the everyday experiences of the most vulnerable learners in our education system and the forces contouring failure and success in the classroom. In this most divisive age of social politics and neoliberal agendas, Johnson, Pratt-Johnson, and their colleagues have sought to build a better world through the telling of everyday actions on both large and small scales. This new addition to the literature on social justice in education shines a much-needed light on the misguided logic of violence, exploitation, and selfishness that undergirds the intersections of poverty and early childhood education.

References

Shields, C., Bogotch, I., & Tooms, A. (2007, November). *Combating the backlash to social justice: Educational leaders embracing the grey-international community-building sessions*. Arlington, VA: University Council for Educational Administration.

Shoho, A., Merchant, B., & Lugg, C. (2005). Seeking a common language. In F. W. English (Ed.), *The Sage handbook of educational leadership, advances in theory leadership, and practice*. Thousand Oaks, CA: Sage Education.

Tooms, A. K., & Boske, C. (Eds.). (2010). *Bridge leadership: Connecting educational leadership and social justice to improve schools*. Charlotte, NC: Information Age Publishing.

Acknowledgments

"One finger cannot lift a pebble." The Hopi proverb metaphorically and succinctly states the collaborative nature of editing a scholarly volume. There is also a large dose of trust that all will be completed as dreamed of so many months ago when we affixed our names to a contract. We are indebted to the following people who helped to make the road from page one to index a travelable one:

Alex Masulis, Senior Editor, Routledge/Taylor & Francis

Lauren Frankfurt, Editorial Assistant, Routledge

Conrado "Bobby" Gempesaw, President, St. John's University

Michael R. Sampson, Dean, The School of Education, St. John's University

Autumn Tooms Cyprès, Associate Dean for Graduate Studies, The School of Education, St. John's University

Robert A. Mangione, Provost and Vice President for Academic Affairs, St. John's University

Contributors

The Editors

Bonnie Johnson earned her Ph.D. from the University of Wisconsin-Madison. In addition to this edited volume, she is the author and co-author of seven books that can be found in over 3,800 libraries around the world. Professor Johnson has also written numerous juried journal articles and book chapters; over 200 instructional texts for elementary, middle school, high school, and adult learners; instructional computer programs; and the monthly newspaper column, *Dr. Bonnie Johnson . . . on Words*. She was co-nominated for the Best Education Book of the Year by the Association of American Publishers, was named an Eminent Literacy Scholar by *The e-Journal of Literacy and Social Responsibility*, and was a recipient of the University of Wisconsin's Distinguished Teacher of Teachers Award. Dr. Johnson is the editor of *The Reading Professor*, an international juried journal. Her research addresses social inequalities in education, high-stakes testing and the school accountability movement, the impact of poverty on vocabulary acquisition, and word origins/etymologies.

Yvonne Pratt-Johnson is Professor of Education and Chair of the Department of Education Specialties. Her teaching and research interests include first and second-language acquisition, literacy development for first and second-language learners, and issues associated with English-based creoles and the teaching of dialect-different students within a "standard English" instructional context. Dr. Pratt-Johnson has presented conference papers and conducted workshops on five continents, published articles in numerous national and international education journals, contributed chapters to books, and received major academic awards and honors. Her four Fulbright-Hays Awards have enabled her to take groups of New York City school teachers to Vietnam (2011, 2013) and to India (2015, 2017), both of which are points of origin for large and growing contingents of New York City public school students. Dr. Pratt-Johnson holds an Ed.D. (Spanish Education/TESOL) from Teachers College, Columbia University.

The Contributors

Sandra Schamroth Abrams has published scholarly articles in the Journal of Adolescent & Adult Literacy, Teachers College Record, Journal of Literacy Research, and The Reading Teacher. Dr. Abrams is the author of Integrating Virtual and Traditional Learning in 6–12 Classrooms: A Layered Literacies Approach to Multimodal Meaning Making (Routledge), co-editor of Bridging Literacies with Videogames (Sense), co-author of Managing Educational Technology: School Partnerships and Technology Integration (Routledge), and co-author of Conducting Qualitative Research of Learning in Online Spaces (SAGE).

Joan Ball holds a Ph.D. in International Business Management, an M.S. in Organizational Leadership, and a B.A. in Economics. Dr. Ball has a particular interest in how micro-businesses and individuals in transition might benefit from access to service design strategies, tools, and techniques. Her research, teaching, and consulting work focus on service design, consumer behavior, and how best to create service systems and processes that result in social impact and human well-being.

Harold T. Broderick, Doctor of Jurisprudence, served as a Detective-Investigator in the New York City Police Department where he earned the New York City Police Department's Medal for Valor. He was a first responder to the World Trade Center attacks on September 11, 2001. Dr. Broderick's research focuses on organized crime, juvenile justice, and the sociology of gang culture. He teaches courses in the Division of Criminal Justice, Legal Studies, and Homeland Security.

Fabienne T. Cadet earned a Ph.D. in Business Administration from Hampton University. She has been a Senior Marketing Manager and a Senior Market Analyst in the corporate arena. Dr. Cadet conducts research in social media marketing, consumer behavior, global marketing, and branding.

Elizabeth Chase earned an Ed.D. from Teachers College, Columbia University. She worked for 15 years in the Harlem and Bronx public schools. Dr. Chase's research examines teacher education and alternative understandings of student achievement. Her most recent article on counternarratives of educational success for young mothers was published in *Educational Studies*.

Autumn Tooms Cyprès is the Associate Dean for Research and Graduate Studies in the School of Education. Dr. Cyprès's research has been nationally recognized via the Paula Silver Case Award and the William J. Davis Award. She has published numerous scholarly articles and authored books that examine the politics of leadership within the professoriate. Dr. Cyprès was the founding director of the Leadership Academy at the University of Tennessee.

Conrado "Bobby" Gempesaw is the President of the three New York City campuses (i.e., Manhattan, Queens, Staten Island); the Rome, Italy campus; and the academic locations of Paris, France; Limerick, Ireland; Seville, Spain; and Hauppauge, New York that comprise St. John's University. Dr. Gempesaw's fields of research include marketing and international trade, financial simulation analysis, and higher education administration; he has written over 100 scholarly journal articles in those areas. Dr. Gempesaw earned a Ph.D. in Agricultural Economics from Penn State University and was recognized by Penn with the 2017 Penn State Graduate School Alumni Society Lifetime Achievement Award.

Donald R. McClure holds a Ph.D. from Michigan State University. Dr. McClure has taught in Louisiana, Illinois, and Ireland. His research interests span the areas of social studies education and international education. He explores how students from diverse backgrounds make sense of citizenship, national identity, and national belonging.

Robert A. Mangione served as Dean of the College of Pharmacy and Health Sciences prior to his appointment as Provost and Vice President for Academic Affairs. Dr. Mangione has served as the editor of the *New York State Journal of Pharmacy* and as a contributing editor to *Children's Hospital Quarterly* and *U. S. Pharmacist*. He also served for a decade as a professional member of the New York State Board of Pharmacy.

Nancy P. Morabito earned a Ph.D. from Vanderbilt University. She has taught in the disciplines of biology, anatomy, and physiology. Her current work focuses on pre-service and in-service STEM teacher development. Dr. Morabito also conducts research on pre-service teacher learning in extended clinical placements through the Residency Internship for St. John's Educators (R.I.S.E.) program which engages pre-service teachers in year-long student teaching experiences.

Daniel Ness holds a Ph.D. from Columbia University's Department of Mathematics, Science, and Technology. He has authored numerous articles on mathematics development and spatial and geometric thinking. Dr. Ness has developed assessment techniques for diagnosing mathematical and scientific thinking. He recently co-edited *Alternatives to Privatizing Public Education and Curriculum: A Festschrift in Honor of Dale D. Johnson* (Routledge) and co-authored *Spatial Intelligence: Why It Matters from Birth through the Lifespan* (Routledge).

Anthony Bayani Rodriguez earned his Ph.D. from the University of Southern California. His research areas include the sociology of knowledge, decolonial social movements, and 21st-century humanism. He is currently a scholar-in-residence at the Schomburg Center for Research in Black Culture.

Dan Rubin holds a Ph.D. in Business from Baruch College where he earned the John A. Elliott Teaching Award. His research focuses on consumer memory and the unconscious effects of packaging and retailer environment on brand choice and preference. He currently teaches classes in the Marketing Department.

Michael R. Sampson is the Dean of the School of Education. He is an internationally recognized authority in the field of literacy and a *New York Times* best-selling author of 30 books for children, including the classic *Chicka, Chicka 1, 2, 3*. Under Dr. Sampson's leadership, university programs have won prestigious honors such as the Christa McAuliffe Award for Exemplary Program in Teacher Education from the American Association of State Colleges and Universities.

Caitlin Stehling, Pharm.D., taught courses in the Department of Clinical Health Professions at St. John's University. Dr. Stehling's research interests include pediatric critical care, emergency medicine, pulmonology, and medication safety. She recently accepted a position as a Pharmacist Specialist at Children's Healthcare of Atlanta.

1 Technology

Factors Behind the Digital Divide

Bonnie Johnson and Yvonne Pratt-Johnson

Introduction

Rancid butter, hermetically sealed, torrential downpour, and *green grass* are *collocations,* words that are often seen or heard together. *Digital divide* is moving toward the linguistic category of collocation. In 1994, *LASIK, spoiler alert,* and *supersize* entered English; so did *digital divide.* Its definition: "the economic, educational, and social inequalities between those who have computers and online access and those who do not" (Merriam-Webster, 2017). Words and word pairs come and go; the obsolete *gandygut* was a person who ate in a gluttonous way; *swarf penny* was money paid to castle guards (Sperling, 1977). Some words change meanings; *lunch,* as defined in Samuel Johnson's 1755 *Dictionary,* meant the amount of food a person could hold in one hand (Johnson & Johnson, 2011). Metcalf (2002) stated that it takes about two generations to know if a word has taken a permanent place in our vocabulary. We sadly predict that if economic circumstances do not change for many young children, *digital divide* will still be in use 40 years hence.

Mouse Problem

We have seen the *digital divide* in our underfunded classrooms: computers old and clumsy enough to be in a museum of history, and money spent on software only if higher test scores were promised by sales personnel. A "mouse problem," as described by a harried district educational technologist, was not a malfunctioning computer device; it was a problem caused by unchecked school rodents chewing through our computer cables. Even when schools have up-to-date devices and software, an Education Week Research Center study showed that, "Teachers in high-poverty schools are consistently less likely than their counterparts to say they've received technology-integration training" (Herold, 2017, p. 3). There are only so many dollars to go around.

Lessons from First-Grade Social Studies

Most six- and seven-year-olds learn that food, clothing, and shelter comprise the basic needs of families. These social studies topics are discussed in the contexts of home, school, and neighborhood. This approach to teaching social studies is referred to as the *expanding environments* pattern where units of study begin with concepts familiar to children and, throughout the years, widen to include ever-more distant environments, concluding with world regions by Grade 8 (Welton, 2005). Those who have spent any time with young children know that they have difficulties with time and distance. The mention of 1861 or 565 miles would draw looks of confusion from young children or would be ignored by them. Discussions of places and conditions close to home are developmentally appropriate for young children because they have concrete examples of these places and conditions—they live in them. This chapter will follow the food, clothing, and shelter framework to examine the daily living experiences of young children that contribute to the digital divide. To eliminate wordiness and clumsiness, the pronoun *we* will be used to describe personal experiences; one or both of us taught in the conditions discussed below.

Food: Data Plan or Dinner?

Happy Birthday

Other than an initial introduction, we met bussing trays. St. John's University in New York City sponsors shuttles to a soup kitchen where University administrators, faculty, staff, and students volunteer to help with lunchtime duties. Our task was to gather plastic trays after the "guests" were finished eating and then take the trays to the man who washed them. We also handed out "extras" to the guests; donated hummus packets ("use by" dates expired) were the extras that day. Amid the crowded, large, unadorned room was a child—around the age of two—in a stroller. As the line formed and meals were dished up, colleagues were told not to give out generous portions because the supply was limited. During the meal, some harsh words were exchanged among a few guests. The woman-in-charge squelched the exchanges. It was a guest's birthday, so the woman-in-charge played "Happy Birthday" on a cassette recorder. One elderly man danced alone. As the two-year-old's table mates returned from the line with their trays, the eating began. There were no interactions with the child; people were hungry and were there to eat. When everyone had been served, guests could line up for their hummus extras, and after that could line up against a wall for seconds if there was any food left over.

Eitzen, Zinn, and Smith (2009) wrote, "The school is analogous to a conveyor belt, with people of all social classes getting on at the same time but leaving the belt in accordance with social class—the lower the class, the shorter the ride" (p. 489). We do not see all children toddle onto the belt at the same time. As the child in the stroller, who ate nothing while we were there, quietly took in her surroundings, other children her age were spending their morning in a starkly different environment.

On our commute from Manhattan to St. John's University's Queens campus, we pass a school that epitomizes Fröbel's *Kindergarten*. The school, located in an affluent section of Manhattan, truly is a *children's garden*. The spacious, bright rooms are filled with enticing materials: expensive blocks sets, art materials of all kinds, carts of children's picture books, puppets, and so much more. Children's plants, with pupil-decorated pots, grow in the windows. The children have music, movement, "cooking," and Spanish lessons. Although no media are visible from the outside windows, we suspect that parents who pay the $26,600 per year (mornings only) tuition for their two-year-olds expect at least introductory, developmentally appropriate lessons on technology. By first grade, all pupils in the school receive their own electronic devices for classroom use. Nutritious snacks are provided by the school.

Weathering is usually applied to rocks and old structures that have endured outdoor exposure. For do-it-yourselfers, paint can be purchased to add a weathered look to newish wood. The paint, report some websites, adds charm—character. Geronimus (1992; Geronimus, Hicken, Keene, & Bound, 2006) used the word *weathering*, however, to describe what happens to poor adults—especially along racial/ethnic differences—as they live lives of poverty. There is nothing charming about human weathering caused by poverty, and the effects caused by weathering can persist even when children's environments change as they grow older. Lewin (2005) described how the effects of poverty linger. Della Mae Justice, the subject of Lewin's writing, moved from a poor household when young to one with more funds. Justice said:

> I didn't know much about the world, and I was always afraid of making a wrong move. When we had a school trip for chorus, we went to a restaurant. I ordered a club sandwich, but when it came with those toothpicks on either end, I didn't know how to eat it, so I just sat there, staring at it and starving, and said I didn't feel well.
>
> (p. 66)

Educators see the beginning of the weathering process in the early years, and it begins with working among hungry children. It is no revelation that there are hungry children in America. We have taught them. Some of our pupils were so hungry that they licked their free breakfast and free lunch trays; there are no finicky eaters in a low-income school. We have taught pupils who did not want to go home on Friday afternoons because they knew that there would be no food again until Monday morning's free school breakfast.

Teachers and administrators in underfunded schools routinely pull out their wallets to buy food for pupils. One of those teachers said, "I can assure you that I had students who came into my classroom without having eaten anything since lunch the previous day" (Walker, 2013, pp. 1–2). A Colorado teacher spoke about a student in her class:

He wears size XXL shirts to hide what we all know is an emaciated frame. A couple of weeks ago, he used a plastic bag—stretched out to its full length—as a belt. He says he doesn't get to choose the size of clothes he gets so he makes do with what he has. He tells me I don't have to buy him food, but I do anyway, because he needs it. He always takes it.

(Strauss, 2015, p. 3)

Statistics on child hunger are not difficult to find. The United States Department of Agriculture Economic Research Service (USDA ERS) (2017) reported that in 2016, there were 6.5 million children who lived in "food-insecure households" (p. 4). "Food-insecure" is a euphemism for hunger and is defined by the USDA as "insufficient money or other resources for food" (p. 2). There are two categories of food insecurity: low food security and very low food security. These categories, with their descriptions, mean one thing to us: children go hungry. Not all of the millions of children counted by the USDA ERC live in urban communities; even a relatively small community such as Green Bay, Wisconsin (population 105,139; 2016 estimate, U.S. Census Bureau) has four food pantries. Green Bay's neighboring town, De Pere, has its own food pantry for a population of 24,893 (FoodPantries.org, 2017). Each numeral represents a human being. The adage, "Statistics represent faces with the tears wiped off" (Rank, 2004, p. 37) comes to mind.

Child hunger becomes an even more serious situation as summer begins. Some schools, for the past several years, have been serving free breakfast and free lunch during summer months; a "slice of meat, a biscuit, orange juice and milk" were served at one Louisiana school where a coordinator noted, "Some of the children may not have breakfast or lunch if we didn't provide it for them" (Wilson, 2004). In Tennessee, a school bus travels with summer lunches for hungry children. On one particular day each sack lunch contained celery sticks (two ounces), canned oranges (four ounces), a bologna sandwich, and chocolate milk. The food costs were supported by the USDA, but as with most freebies, there are rules attached: no seconds, no taking the food home, and the especially stingy "no extra milks" (Saslow, 2013, p. 3).

The USDA uses the term *food deserts* for areas of the country that do not have enough grocery stores or farmers' markets to sell healthy foods to residents (American Nutrition Association, 2015). Some years ago, Cassese (2006) wrote about the lack of supermarket chains and sometimes higher prices in low-income areas. Professor of Marketing, Richard Rauch, explained:

There's a perception [among chains] that low-income areas are difficult . . . They believe you can't make a large amount of money because people mainly buy basic items and they don't buy the higher-margin items . . . If you had more competition there, it would change things.

(Cassese, 2006, p. A28)

When stores are scarce, merchants can charge higher prices. One day on our way home from St. John's University, we noticed the price of avocados in a low-income area—a food desert—in Queens. Each avocado, non-organic, somewhat shriveled, and not much bigger than a chicken egg, was priced at $2.50. On that same day, we saw non-organic, not-on-sale, larger and plumper avocados for sale in an affluent neighborhood in Manhattan; the price was $1.49 each. *The Other America: Poverty in the United States* was written in 1962 and was thought to be an impetus for President Lyndon B. Johnson's War on Poverty, a War that was not "fought to victory" (Shipler, 2004, 2005, p. 6). In *The Other America*, Michael Harrington refers to economically poor people as being "fat with hunger, for that is what cheap foods do" (p. 2). For $2.50, the price of a puny food-desert avocado, a family can buy two boxes of filling, generic macaroni and cheese dinners and still have money left over.

When families grapple with not having enough to eat, there is less money—or no money—for data plans. Some children stand outside schools in the evenings so that they can use the schools' "wireless hot spots" to complete their homework; the children have no home Internet services (Kang, 2016, pp. 1–5). Other children rely on Wi-Fi in school buses or access the Internet in fast-food restaurants so that they can do their homework. Some students, as our pupils did, use the technology in public libraries, but they must often wait in line, as our pupils had to do, and walking home from the library in the dark can be a frightening, unsafe experience for young children.

The International Literacy Association (ILA) (2017), in their brief, "Overcoming the Digital Divide," pointed out an additional complication and burden that low-income children face: teachers who teach children from low socioeconomic backgrounds know that there is no Internet access in their homes, so they do not use the technology in their lessons. The ILA also noted that even if students from low-income families own a mobile device, that device is not sufficient for the completion of many assignments such as longer narratives than those completed in school.

Clothing: "Change into What?"

Those who work in low-income schools know that many children come to school wearing thin T-shirts without jackets and coats on icy days, pants that are rolled up several times to allow for yearly growth, and ill-fitting shoes with holes in the soles exposing tattered socks (see Johnson & Johnson, 2006). If children lose an article of clothing—or even a pair of eyeglasses—they know better than to ask for another. "Lost and Found" boxes in low-income schools are not stuffed with items. A trip to Goodwill, not Wal-Mart, is a family shopping outing. Some schools have "stores" where the pupils can "buy" donated clothing with "money" earned through regular attendance and respectable deportment (Riley, 2012).

The woman who drove the summer food bus mentioned above made her first stop one day where five siblings had gathered. She noticed that they were wearing the sauce-stained clothes from food served the day before. When the driver asked the children about changing their clothes that day, one of them replied, "Into what?" (Saslow, 2013, p. 3).

It is not uncommon for teachers and staff who work in low-income schools to wash and dry their pupils' clothing—in school and in their own homes—because the children's dwellings have no washers or dryers. In one of our former schools, a second-grader was living in a pop-up trailer with no running water or electricity. In another school district, a family of 11 (grandma and grandpa included) were living in tents. "The youngest little guy had come to school, and his clothes were in bad shape and they were really short," said a school staff member. "That's just one story. We have so many," reported another (Frenette, 2014, pp. 22–23).

Some schools keep donated clothes in a supply closet so that children can change into clean clothes while the clothes they slept in and wore to school that day can be washed and dried between classes (see Albright, 2014, 2015). Although the students were not young children, one of our graduate students took home his middle-school's basketball team's uniforms to wash after games because the school had one set of uniforms, and the students had no washers or dryers at home.

Those who doubt reports of pupils who are inadequately dressed for the weather, who sleep in the same clothes they wear to school, whose laundry is washed in a kitchen sink or by school personnel, need to spend some time in an underfunded school. The schools are not difficult to locate. It would not take much time to convince skeptics that there is a lack of clean, weather- and size-appropriate clothing for many pupils. Perhaps the skeptics would think twice about praising and rewarding "blue ribbon schools" (with their sophisticated technology) where healthy, well-fed, well-dressed, and well-tutored children score high on state and national tests, and where back-to-school purchases might include $195 headbands, $572 backpacks (Abrams, 2016), and up-to-date electronic devices.

Shelter: "Duct Tape and Chewing Gum"

The Home

Drives through neighborhoods where economically poor pupils live show homes and apartments with windows boarded up (no money for glass replacement), jalopies (no money for towing or repair), and often darkness at night (electricity turned off due to unpaid bills). A look inside some of the dwellings might reveal mouse dander, roach infestations, and mold—all of which can trigger asthma attacks (Carroll, 2014). Some Americans lack proper plumbing. Tavernise (2016) wrote:

Nearly half a million households in the United States lack the basic dignity of hot and cold running water, a bathtub or shower, or a working flush toilet, according to the Census Bureau. The absence has implications for public health in the very population that is the most vulnerable.

(p. 1)

If there is no money for electricity, plumbers, or exterminators, it is doubtful that there are family funds for up-to-date electronic devices. There certainly is no money for four-day computer/robotics/STEM camps for children that run in the summers for hundreds of dollars (see, for example, UW-Green Bay Robotics and STEM Camps, Summer Camps Brochure, 2017). Slots in these camps fill, and all of us know who are attending.

Most of the parents and guardians of the children whom we taught worked at least one minimum-wage job. Some pupils' parents were in prison, a few serving life sentences for murder. Other parents were just absent. One pupil reported, "Every day she drunk or gone," when asked if he could get extra help at home with his math. Our graduate students, former and current, who teach in low-income schools report all-too-familiar home conditions: gangs whose members sometimes include pupils' parents and older siblings; alcohol and drug abuse by parents, guardians, and older siblings; sleeping on mats or two/three to a bed; utilities turned off and on. The conditions take their toll on young children who have no say in their socioeconomic status. One does not have to be well off financially to be a good parent, but having enough money to provide a healthy, habitable dwelling with up-to-date electronic gadgets and gizmos requires funds.

The School

It is relatively easy—in comparison to teaching in an underfunded school for a brief period of time—to write sets of standards that all children are expected to achieve. Contemporary education is awash in these standards. Additional funding to meet the standards is scarce, though, so more and more low-income pupils fail to reach grade-level expectations. One Delaware educator referred to the state as behaving like "a high-grade bully" in its demands (Albright, 2014, 2015). There is no shortage of high-grade bullies, at all levels, who talk tough about clamping down on "failing" schools and increasing academic "rigor." Media examples of this hard-line stance abound (see Johnson, 2017).

Schools take a lot of blame for societal ills, but they are some of the few places economically poor children can feel secure despite the dangerous neighborhoods where the schools are located. Within school walls that serve economically poor children, teachers and administrators provide toiletries such as toothbrushes and small holiday gifts in attempts to counteract homelessness, domestic and neighborhood violence, apartment overcrowding, and other weathering factors (Harris, 2016). Most public schools rely on local tax dollars for their support. The state might contribute some money, and the federal government as well, but community tax dollars largely dictate levels of school funding, so conditions in schools resemble the conditions of the environments in which children live. Leaky roofs, malfunctioning sprinkler systems, structurally unsound foundations, exploding boilers, and other physical-plant problems occasionally make the headlines of local media; however, no connection is drawn between providing decent places for learning and closing any kind of gap: literacy gap, math gap, science proficiency gap, or digital divide (Brown, 2016). Politicians talk about repairing roads and bridges as safety measures, and those repairs are vital, but as Brown noted, during the weekdays, "some 56 million students and teachers—more than one-sixth of the U.S. population" (p. 1) are in school buildings. One school maintenance mechanic, in describing the school in which he works, said, "This school has been patched together with duct tape and chewing gum" (Providence Journal, 2017, p. 1).

A Promising Solution to the Digital Divide: Wraparound Environments

In seeking solutions to ameliorating inequalities in the early years, some cities and states have shown an understanding of the interconnectedness of it all. The State of Connecticut offers "wraparound services" to schools that include, for example:

- family engagement, parent leadership, and adult education
- extended learning opportunities and youth development
- physical, dental, and mental health programs and social services
- afterschool, mentoring, and tutoring programs
- early childhood development
- full utilization of federal and state nutrition programs (breakfast, lunch, supper, snack, and Healthy Food Certification).

(Connecticut State Department of Education [CSDE], 2017, p. 1)

The CSDE, in explaining partnerships with existing community resources, pointed out that the wraparound services would use schools as the "hubs of the community, accessible to children and families, including evenings and weekends, as needed" (p.1). The services are no more than what economically privileged children receive; food, medical and dental care, tutoring, and early childhood education, for starters. After all, these children, despite economic circumstances, must all take the same state and federal tests.

New York City's Community Schools Initiative reflects a similar understanding of the interconnections among factors that undergird school success.

The Initiative offers vision and dental care, counseling services, afterschool programs, and more to needy schools. New York City has been a leader in universal pre-kindergarten, and that is an admirable step in supporting families who cannot afford to send their children to such programs.

"How much will this cost the taxpayer?" is a perennial question that arises when these programs are announced. For each New York City school that is a part of the community-based program, the cost is approximately $350,000 per year for the services (Taylor, 2017). That's a lot of money, but a pittance when one considers what can happen to children when they do not have even the basic resources to succeed in school. We have seen the hunger, the decayed teeth, the neighborhood violence, the lack of school resources, and have heard the persistent harping about raising test scores, and we have seen what has happened to many of our former pupils when there are no jobs and hopes of finding employment have long dried up. In hard-nosed economic terms, what are the costs of supporting economically unproductive members of our society—in even the most modest estimations? More than the $350,000 per school (divided by numerous pupils) per year? As Horace (65–8 BC) wrote, "Your own property is at stake when your neighbor's house is on fire" (Rank, 2004, p. 85), and if early inequalities must be considered in such a bottom-line manner to draw attention to and attempt to alleviate the underlying problems, so be it.

Gladwell (2003) pointed out, "If schools were factories, America would have solved the education problem a century ago" (p. 34). Perhaps Gladwell is correct in some regards, but "the education problem" will not be solved until the complex problem of child poverty is addressed. Feelings about why people are poor can be established before the onset of adulthood. Johnson, Johnson, Farenga, and Ness (2008) asked a group of fifth- to tenth-grade students, who came from financially privileged backgrounds, why people were poor. Here are a few of their responses:

> *Jake, seventh grader:* Because they make poor decisions. They often come from bad families or broken homes. A lot of the time they are lazy.
> *Samantha, fifth grader:* People are poor because they don't work hard enough to make money.
> *Valerie, sixth grader:* Because they don't work hard.
> *Chase, eighth grader:* There is a lot of poverty in the world, and I strongly believe that the main reason is that people do not work hard enough, they are lazy and do not have the motivation to better themselves.
> *Lynn, tenth grader:* Because they are too lazy to get off their butts and get a job . . . They caused it because if they really cared about being poor, then they would get a job.
> *Summer, eighth grader:* I believe people are poor because of laziness.
> (p. 61)

None of the young people mentioned death of wage earners, staggering medical bills, minimum-wage jobs, racism, or any other factors that can contribute to poverty. None thought twice about their bright futures. Nathan, for example, said:

> I am going to go to college; there has never been any other option for me . . . I do not know the exact college that I want to go to, but the college will be a prestigious one . . . my career will be in the realm of business and law.
>
> (Johnson, Johnson, Farenga, & Ness, 2008, p. 57)

If the attitudes of the young people above reflect those of their affluent parents, we have more than a digital divide to ameliorate.

The chapters in this volume follow ten of lexicographer Barbara Ann Kipfer's (1998, p. v) delineation of broad subject areas of knowledge: technology, society and social institutions, mathematics and measurements, physical sciences, business and economics, history, the arts, sports and recreation, life sciences, and earth sciences and geography. The category of religion is addressed in the Preface. An additional chapter on literacy has been included because of its importance in the early years and beyond. All chapters are written by multidisciplinary faculty members and two administrators at St. John's University, New York City.

It is not common for academics to spend thought and time on fields outside their areas of expertise. As Rank (2004) pointed out, "Given the volumes of information generated these days surrounding virtually any subject, one's area of expertise is often narrowed by necessity" (p. vi). This specialization of knowledge and talent, however, has, as Rank noted, caused academicians who focus on one tree to "lose sight of the forest" (p. vi). Those in the academy know the expectations of their discipline, the politics within the discipline, and the ways to secure safe positions within the discipline; to step outside these parameters is not self-serving. Giroux (2006) wrote, however, that when academics do not take roles in "lessening human suffering" (p. 64), they "publish while others perish" (Zinn, 2001, p. 178 in Giroux, 2006, p. 64). The Foreword, Preface, and chapters that follow are written by academics who have invested thought and words in the hopes of aiding our most vulnerable. They have our gratitude and respect.

References

Abrams, R. (2016, August 29). Back-to-school divide: $195 headbands and $1 glue sticks. *The New York Times*. Retrieved from www.nytimes.com.

Albright, M. (2014, 2015). Fixing Delaware's troubled schools. Retrieved from www.delawareonline.com.

American Nutrition Association. (2015). USDA defines food deserts. Retrieved from http://americannutritionassociation.org/newsletter/usda-defines-food-deserts.

Brown, E. (2016, March 23). Report finds massive under-investment in nation's school buildings. *The Washington Post*. Retrieved from www.washingtonpost.com.

Carroll, L. (2014). Mold, mice and zip codes: Inside the childhood asthma epidemic. Retrieved from http://inplainsight.nbcnews.com.

Cassese, S. (2006, February 22). Marketing or discrimination? *Newsday*, p. A28.

Connecticut State Department of Education. (2017). Wraparound services and closing the achievement gap. Retrieved from www.sde.ct.gov.

Eitzen, D. S., Zinn, M. B., & Smith, K. E. (2009). *Social problems* (11th ed.). New York: Pearson.

FoodPantries.org. (2017). Wisconsin cities. Retrieved from www.foodpantries.org.

Frenette, L. (2014). Out in the cold. *NYSUT United*, *5*(1), 22–23.

Geronimus, A. T. (1992). The weathering hypothesis and the health of African-American women and infants: Evidence and speculation. *Ethnicity and Disease*, Summer, *2*(3), 207–221.

Geronimus, A. T., Hicken, M., Keene, D., & Bound, J. (2006). "Weathering" and age patterns of allostatic load scores among blacks and whites in the United States. *American Journal of Public Health*, *96*(5), 826–833.

Giroux, H. A. (2006). Higher education under siege: Implications for public intellectuals. *Thought & Action*, *22*, 63–78.

Gladwell, M. (2003, September 15). Making the grade. *The New Yorker*, 31, 34.

Harrington, M. (1962, 1969, 1981, 1993). *The other America: Poverty in the United States*. New York: Touchstone.

Harris, E. A. (2016, June 6). *Where nearly half of pupils are homeless, school aims to be teacher, therapist, even Santa*. Retrieved from www.nytimes.com.

Herold, B. (2017, June 12). *Poor students face digital divide in how teachers learn to use tech*. Retrieved from www.edweek.org.

International Literacy Association (ILA). (2017). Literacy leadership brief: Overcoming the digital divide: Four critical steps. Retrieved from literacyworldwide.org/position-statements.

Johnson, B. (2017). "Every day she drunk or gone": Poverty, persuasion, peddlers, and privatization. In D. Ness & S. Farenga (Eds.), *Alternatives to privatizing public education and curriculum: A Festschrift in honor of Dale D. Johnson*. New York: Routledge.

Johnson, D. D., & Johnson, B. (2006). *High stakes: Poverty, testing, and failure in American Schools* (2nd ed.). New York: Rowman & Littlefield.

Johnson, D. D., & Johnson, B. (2011). *Words: The foundation of literacy*. Boulder, CO: Westview/Perseus Books Group.

Johnson, D. D., Johnson, B., Farenga, S., & Ness, D. (2008). *Stop high-stakes tesing*.New York: Rowman & Littlefield.

Kang, C. (2016, February 22). Bridging a digital divide that leaves schoolchildren behind. *The New York Times*. Retrieved from www.nytimes.com.

Kipfer, B. A. (1998). *The order of things*. New York: Random House.

Lewin, T. (2005). Up from the holler: Living in two worlds, at home in neither. In Correspondents of *The New York Times* (Contributors). *Class matters*. New York: Henry Holt.

Merriam-Webster. (2017). Definition of digital divide, first known use. Retrieved from www.merriam-webster.com.

Metcalf, A. (2002). *Predicting new words*. Boston, MA: Houghton Mifflin.

Providence Journal. (2017, June 5). Editorial: Fix R.I.'s crumbling schools. Retrieved from www.providencejournal.com/opinion.

Rank, M. R. (2004). One nation, underprivileged: Why American poverty affects us all. New York: Oxford University Press.

Riley, C. (2012, September 18). Children in poverty: No shoes. *Springfield News-Leader*. Retrieved from www.news-leader.com.

Saslow, E. (2013, July 6). In rural Tennessee, a new way to help hungry children: A bus turned bread truck. *The Washington Post*. Retrieved from http://washingtonpost.com.

Shipler, D. K. (2004, 2005). *The working poor: Invisible in America*. New York: Vintage Books.

Sperling, S. K. (1977). Poplollies and bellicones: A celebration of lost words. Old Saybrook, CT: Konecky & Konecky.

Strauss, V. (2015, January 29). Teacher: I see the difference in educational privilege every day. I live it. I am disgusted by it. *The Washington Post*. Retrieved from http://washingtonpost.com.

Tavernise, S. (2016, September 26). Too poor for proper plumbing: A reality in 500,000 U.S. homes. Retrieved from www.nytimes.com.

Taylor, K. (2017, May 11). De Blasio, expanding an education program, dismisses past approaches. *The New York Times*. Retrieved from www.nytimes.com.

United States Department of Agriculture Economic Research Service (USDA ERS). (2017). Food security status of U. S. households in 2016. Retrieved from www.ers.usda.gov/topics/food-nutrition-assistance/food-security-in-the-us.

UW-Green Bay Robotics & STEM Camps (2017). Summer camps brochure. Retrieved from www.uwgbsummercamps.com.

Walker, T. (2013). Report: Teachers spend $37 every month to help feed hungry students. Retrieved from http://neatoday.org/2013/09/10.

Welton, D. A. (2005). Children and their world: Strategies for teaching social studies (8th ed.). Boston, MA: Houghton Mifflin.

Wilson, L. (2004, June 4). Schools feed children meals over summer break. *The News Star*. Retrieved from www.thenewsstar.com.

Zinn, H. (2001). *On history*. New York: Seven Stories Press.

2 Mathematics and Measurements

Young Children Count: Undoing Reverse Constructivism During Early Childhood Mathematical Experiences

Daniel Ness

Introduction

While the Orwellian use of language has been damaging to education, it has had particularly deleterious effects on young children. Orwellian language is by no means a recent phenomenon in education talk. For example, in the U.S. from the 1950s to the present, we have had "New Math," "A Nation at Risk," "Goals 2000," "No Child Left Behind," and "Race to the Top," to name a few. The list of Orwellian language in education doesn't stop there. These terms are called doublespeak because they are either in the form of euphemism or hyperbole as a means of concealing falsehood or exaggeration. To be sure, who wants "old math"? Are we placing the concern of risk of a nation's education system on the right issues—such as poverty, racism, and sexism? Who would want a child to be left behind? Or race somewhere other than the top?

Orwellian doublespeak can sound too good to be true, and, more often than not, doublespeak initiatives are almost never achieved. For example, the G. W. Bush era's No Child Left Behind set a goal that by 2014, all children in the United States would be performing at the level of "proficient" at grade level.[1] Unfortunately, nothing could be further from the truth. Children of families below the poverty line do not have nearly the resources available to them as do children of families with higher incomes, and therefore are unable to "catch up" to the level of "proficient." Rather, much of what comes of these initiatives are standards, whose developers' aim is to set standardized assessment goals for all children, without consideration of their backgrounds or socioeconomic status (SES). While standards serve as an indicator for the purpose of generalizability, current mathematics standards as a one-size-fits-all arrangement are woefully callous in terms of how they are applied to young children, particularly those from low-income families. Organized educational frameworks, such as standards, are initiated and established by individuals, many of whom are educational administrators and policymakers, who may not necessarily appreciate or recognize the spontaneous nature and individual differences of young children's mathematical thinking and propensities. Most alarmingly, educational policies tend to place poor children at a much greater disadvantage than their more affluent peers because the uniform nature of standards does not account for lack of resources that are primarily unavailable in homes or schools that enroll children from families of low SES backgrounds.

Through the notion of environmental generational amnesia, a term introduced by Kahn (2002), constructivist philosophy—considered by many cognitive theorists and educators as the touchstone of Piaget's theoretical program and a highly progressive forward-thinking approach to education in general and mathematical thinking in particular—is revisited in this chapter. Constructivism is most often discussed or referenced in education and developmental psychology research as a progressive philosophy with optimistic outcomes that develop in all of us from infancy through the lifespan. While constructivism provides a humanistic approach to development and learning, it can also work against progressive development (a process I refer to as reverse constructivism).

In this chapter, it is suggested that in many early childhood settings, particularly those in low-income neighborhoods or those in abject poverty, young children develop mathematical ideas through reverse constructivism—a developmental perspective, like Piagetian constructivism, which maintains that mental schemas that undergird cognitive development adjust and readjust through the processes of assimilation, accommodation, and equilibration. But unlike the constructivist model, in reverse constructivism, knowledge becomes limited and constrained as a result of developing values or constructs in a particular society and in successive generations that are intrinsically associated with high-stakes testing, teaching by rote methods, and unmitigated dependence on digital technologies at the expense of conceptual understanding. This situation is especially dire for children living in poverty who have no alternative but to compete with peers from higher-income families—who therefore have more access to resources—on the same high-stakes assessments that are often used for grade promotion. This chapter continues with an analysis of two early childhood setting scenarios from preschools, which accommodate children from low-income households. These cases exhibit young children's remarkable mathematical propensities and use of invented strategies for solving challenging mathematical problems. The chapter concludes with five strategies that teachers, parents, and education faculty can implement to ensure equity in young children's mathematical experiences.

Language and Educational Sadism

Language can be highly misleading, especially when it is used in euphemistic terms as a means of concealing the essence of reality. As indicated above, terms such as "No Child Left Behind" and "Race to the Top" are euphemisms in education discourse, but those who have used them do so with often pernicious intentions. To be sure, when scratching the surfaces of these federal and state education initiatives—as well as those that preceded and followed them—it becomes more evident that the underlying factor in nearly all them is high-stakes testing. Some have even posited that such terms lead to perverse outcomes in education because the intentions of the individuals who use them run counter to the terms' actual meanings (Pinar, 2017; Ravitch, 2013). This problem resonates all the more when considering preschoolers and school-aged children. Pinar (2017) justifiably equates high-stakes testing and other forms of standardized assessment as a form of school reform sadism. His view is based on the draconian measures that many state officials take, such as those from Louisiana, when they issue legislation that mandates the administration of high-stakes tests in order to determine grade promotion, even as early as kindergarten (Johnson & Johnson, 2006). Pinar's point is that education policymakers are either unaware of the inequities in schooling or are deliberately or instinctively taking pleasure in the travails of children struggling in high-stakes situations—regardless of their families' socioeconomic backgrounds. Without question, children of poor families suffer immensely when high-stakes testing is a factor in their lives, especially when high rates of neighborhood crime and lack of health and dental care take precedence over a test grade.

Resource Distribution to Poor Young Children—Or the Lack Thereof

High-stakes testing is not only a mainstay in post-industrial societies; it threatens the livelihood and very existence of poor children in developing countries, too. It is important to note, then, that of the world's population in extreme poverty, nearly 400 million fall under the age of 18. Of these, approximately 250 million are 9 years or younger—the period of human development that generally falls under early childhood (UNICEF, 2016). Since the mid-1970s, with the increasing level of perceived crisis regarding ability in literacy and quantitative reasoning came a sense of urgency among education officials in countries throughout the world to test children for the purpose of periodic cross-national comparison. This hype spawned the creation and development of three international testing programs—Programme for International Student Assessment (PISA), the Progress in International Reading Literacy Study (PIRLS), and Trends in International Mathematics and Science Study (TIMSS)—initiatives that have become fixtures in the international testing scene since the onset of the 21st century (Smith, 2016). Children—and young children in particular—have been alienated by these developments, so much so that education officials in developing countries ignore the needs of children altogether. Many children in poverty who are disaffected or cannot attend school due to distance and lack of resources often turn to grueling and appalling child labor work such as quarry mining, farming, garbage picking, leather tanning, or joining militia (Cho, Fang, Tayur, & Xu, 2015; Parker, 2007; Wessells, 2009). In these regions, children in poverty and their families have had little, if any, connection with formal schooling, and the connections they do have are those in which methods of teaching and instruction involve rote, mechanical techniques and high-stakes assessments that serve to keep children in or out of formal education. This form of educational institutionalization severely marginalizes children in developing nations in that they lack the time and resources, both physical and financial, for succeeding in school. Many children, and their parents or caregivers for that matter, are often unaware of what an education can provide in terms of social and physical capital and future success.

In the U.S., when it comes to progressive (i.e., constructivist) learning and the provision of time for engaging in creative, challenging, and stimulating activities, it is known from past and current research that, in comparison with their middle- and upper-income peers, poor children get the short end of the educational stick (Johnson & Johnson, 2006). There is no doubt that across-the-board federal funding for education has the potential to equalize educational opportunities for all students. But in the current political and educational Zeitgeist, federal funding of this kind seems far from reality. An examination of U.S. court decisions brings to light the challenges and adversities that have unfolded throughout history to the present. In this regard, de jure segregation and de facto segregation have played shameful roles in American education history. As stated in Johnson, Johnson, Farenga, and Ness (2008), "De jure segregation is segregation created by law. De facto segregation is segregation according to factual data" (p. 105). Many examples of de jure segregation exist: *Roberts v. City of Boston* (1850) and *Plessy v. Ferguson* (1896) are two examples of de jure segregation, which made it law to separate black and white students and mandate that they attend different schools. Not until the *Brown v. Board of Education* decision of 1954 did the courts recognize that "separate but equal" was unconstitutional and that there was a grossly unequal distribution of resources favoring mainly white schools.

The 1973 Supreme Court case, *San Antonio Independent School District v. Rodriguez*, concluded that distribution of school funds through property taxes did not violate the Equal Protection Clause of the Fourteenth Amendment. The outcome of this case essentially brought federal sponsorship of equality in education to an end. The problem, however, is that when de jure segregation is declared unconstitutional by the Supreme Court, de facto segregation sets in and eventually becomes a fixture of society. Examples of de facto segregation in today's American education system abound and include, but are not limited to, communities or districts in large metropolitan areas with substandard living quality, high violent crime rates, and sorely limited opportunities for children to engage in natural outdoor activities; de facto segregation is also apparent in towns or cities where more affluent families send their children to private schools or academies that exclude children of families with low incomes. Moreover, the strong push since the 2016 presidential election for allocation of federal funds to corporate entities and charter schools is making matters worse for children living in poverty. It is important to note, then, that limited resources—both physical and financial—have led to disastrous consequences and outcomes for poor children.

Devastating outcomes as a result of poverty also include poor healthcare, dental care, and overall physical wellbeing, and a dearth of social services. For example, different SES classifications have been shown to be correlated with varied levels of brain development. In their study on brain development and poverty, Noble, Norman, and Farah (2005) have shown that, due to lack of exposure to informal educationally related experiences, kindergarten children living in poverty performed worse than middle SES kindergarten children on tasks related to the left perisylvian/language system and the prefrontal/executive system. Based on these results, they suggest that SES is the primary reason for this deficit. More recently, Noble and colleagues (2015) found that SES is strongly correlated with language and executive function. Children of families earning less than $25,000 annually suffer the most. In corroboration with Noble and colleagues, a National Institute of Health (NIH)-funded study by Chin-Lun Hung and his colleagues (2015) suggests that early childhood poverty—given increased numbers of stressors such as anxiety and personal safety in socioeconomically impoverished environments—may lead to neurological impairment.

As indicated in Mariani (2017), Noble and her colleagues are currently in the process of developing a five-year longitudinal, nationwide study that may demonstrate a causal link between brain development and poverty. A total of 1,000 low-income families will be divided into two groups: one group will receive $333 per month ($4,000) per year and the other group will receive $20 per month. Noble and colleagues predict that children in the group receiving the larger amount will benefit in terms of physical health and neurological development similar to that of middle- and upper-income families. If the results are positive, this longitudinal study would be one of the first studies to causally link SES with neurocognitive outcomes. What is promising is that the work of Noble and her colleagues has the potential to show that brain stimulation and neural growth development through exposure to diverse educational experiences in a variety of academic and non-academic situations are always possible and evident when children have greater access to a variety of resources that are typically available to more affluent peers. That is, experience matters. Moreover, programs that work toward eradicating poverty have the most potential of increasing cognitive development. But, unfortunately, political administration and legislation that emphasize cuts to healthcare and other safety net programs that aid the physical, social, psychological, economic, and intellectual wellbeing of all people will lead to devastating outcomes for poor children.

Environmental Generational Amnesia and Reverse Constructivism

Although the meaning of constructivism is difficult to capture in a few sentences or a paragraph, it is possible to generalize one of its main principles;

that is, during the course of cognitive development, humans construct new knowledge based on prior experiences through active engagement in their settings (DeVries & Zan, 1994; Ginsburg & Opper, 1988; Piaget, 1954). As they actively interact in their unique environments, young children implement these prior experiences in both previously occupied and novel activities. During these experiences, they will eventually accommodate new knowledge as they encounter discrepant events—occurrences that are not anticipated by the viewer—that are dependent on the situational contexts of their surroundings.

A commonly held position in Piagetian constructivist philosophy and its use in educational circles is that, in constructivism, intellectual tasks improve in accuracy or complexity over time. So, while children's (and adults') initial conceptions of the world can be misconstrued—namely, those that are often based on preconceptions of reality—children (from the semiotic function period and older) have the potential to hone and re-hone their ideas about the world and their unique environments. For example, a child living in Canada or northern Europe might believe that the further south one travels, the warmer the climate. When the child accommodates the schema that Polar Regions of the earth tend to be much colder than those closer to the equator, the child can be said to have progressed from a preconception to a more accurate theory or understanding of the physical occurrence or phenomenon of global climate.

But what if this new knowledge is not based on reality? What happens when an entire generation develops commonly held beliefs that are not based on fact or evidence drawn from data sources? Might the absence of reality in a conception of an event or phenomenon be a situation of reverse constructivism—that is, when constructivism is not based on fact or evidence? Kahn (2011) provides a useful example of a simple idea that demonstrates what I refer to as reverse constructivism: the rising and setting of the sun. To this day, many of us use cognitive shorthand when we explain daytime hours to be those between sunrise and sunset. Clearly, from both physical and ontological perspectives, the sun neither rises nor sets; rather, the earth rotates as it revolves around the sun. But based on our everyday experiences, we don't see it that way because as humans, we don't construe our reality from the perspective of the macrospatial environment—that is, we are not large enough physically to grapple with reality in astronomical terms.

Perhaps one of the most illuminating discussions on the problem of the reversal of constructivism is that of environmental generational amnesia, a term coined by Kahn (2002) that conveys the idea of an individual's lack of positive experiences in specific environments—those that seem to develop in the wrong direction. Kahn exemplifies environmental generational amnesia in terms of air quality. He states that if people live in a region with poor air quality or water pollution for a lengthy time period, they begin to be desensitized by the harmful consequences, even from nonpoint source (i.e., two or more diffuse sources) pollution (Farenga & Ness, 2007), and will begin to suffer from unanticipated illnesses associated with them. In support, research also suggests that the neighborhood in which a child resides influences social, emotional, and cognitive development that can lead to narrow, misguided conceptualizations of reality (Brooks-Gunn, Duncan, Klebanov, & Sealand, 1993; Leventhal & Brooks-Gunn, 2000). In this regard, Kahn argues that when an entire generation begins to develop conceptions of events or phenomena that are not based on reality, members of that generation develop what he calls environmental generational amnesia. So, it is possible to argue that numerous generations have settled on the idea of sunsets and sunrises and not earth rotations; this is where environmental generational amnesia sets in. But those of us who learn about the 24-hour rotation of the earth as it revolves around the sun know that when we use the terms "sunrise" and "sunset," we are doing so casually, with no intention of deceiving others.

Environmental generational amnesia is more damaging when constructivism fails the individual in such a way that it damages both physical and social environments. In developing the concept of environmental generational amnesia, Kahn draws from Diamond's (2005) concept of landscape amnesia, which describes what happens when subsequent generations of a given culture continue to exploit the land and its growth (trees and plants) for the purpose of building shelter or selling lumber. If we consider the problem of deforestation in Chaco Canyon in present-day New Mexico during the period between 600 and 1200 AD, the first generation of those who inhabited the area and engaged in logging for the primary purpose of heat and shelter might have believed that there would be limited or no extensive harm to the natural environment. However, after several generations, inhabitants of the area most apparently became enculturated in the act of logging because they probably did not realize (or did not have the thought of realizing) what forests actually looked like decades or centuries earlier. As a result, deforestation occurred to the point that woodlands were completely destroyed. In sum, reverse constructivism became a staple of the inhabitants' ways of knowing. In an interview with the Natural Histories Project, Kahn states thus:

> The land above my cabin that I built as a teenager was old growth . . . 30 feet behind the cabin. And over subsequent years it's been logged five times. And each time it was logged, I would walk the land and each time it was logged it was taken down to 11 inches in diameter on 60 degree slopes. And I walked the land and I cried because it's so sad and devastating. But now the problem is that people from the city, when they come up to these sorts of areas, they come and they see trees that are 11 inches in diameter and they think these are really good, healthy, and reasonable forests. What's their calibration? Their calibration is from urban settings or much more devastating settings. So, across generations, as kids come of age in these more degraded conditions,

they calibrate on these and they think that's normal and healthy. And if we don't solve that problem of this environmental generational amnesia, I don't see how we're going to solve the large issues because the problem is that people don't recognize that there is a problem. It's a psychological issue . . . What's the role of psychology in terms of natural history? . . . If we can't recognize the problem, there's no way we're going to solve it.

(Drummond & Steele, 2017)

Kahn is asserting a crucial point: current generations (with exceptions), many from large metropolitan areas, are generally unaware of the essential realities of nature. In his example, healthy trees had diameters much larger than 11 inches—the diameter thought to be "healthy" by current generations visiting the countryside from the city environs. With young children growing up in urban and suburban environments, descendants run the risk of developing environmental generational amnesia. As seen in previous examples, such a trend can lead to devastating consequences in future generations. Kahn also warns against adverse uses of various technologies and media. In raising the issue of technologies, he argues that while electronic technologies can be useful in the course of human development, they can be harmful if children are not, at the same time, engaging with their natural world. In short, technologies can be most helpful if they serve society by connecting children with the outdoors and the natural environment afforded to them.

Also of note in this discussion is the intrinsic link between neurological changes in the brain and children's experiences over time. In the decades following Piaget's death, developmental studies have increasingly shown the manifold nature of constructivism in terms of the unfolding of ideas through one's experiences and its impact on our biology, what Newcombe (2011) refers to as neoconstructivism. In sum, Kahn's position regarding environmental generational amnesia and Newcombe's suggestion of neoconstructivism show that biological factors are inherently intertwined with the way we think— that is, greater diversity of experiences leads to neural imprinting, which thus increases young children's potential in intellectual tasks. Therefore, the eradication of poverty must be a key step in leveling the playing field so that all children can benefit from learning and exploring new and creative ideas.

Reverse Constructivism and Mathematical Thinking

So, it can also be argued that young children who are not provided the opportunities to play and search out the answers to mathematical challenges in their everyday goings-on will eventually fall into the environmental generational amnesia pattern. This is most commonly apparent when children are formally instructed mathematics at the earliest ages. Numerous studies have shown that teaching formal mathematics in early childhood is detrimental to children's conceptualization of mathematics as they become older

(Copley, 2000; Greenes, 1999; Seo & Ginsburg, 2004). It should come as no surprise, then, that children who do not have informal experiences in mathematics do not often engage in the kind of imagination that is important for success in mathematics in secondary school and beyond.

Although calculator use is a fascinating tool that has the potential of increasing the possibilities of constructing alternative mathematical models for understanding, it has detrimental effects as well. It is possible to examine the current generation of students in upper elementary school and secondary school in terms of their strengths and weaknesses in mathematics in relation to their dependence on calculators in the mathematics classroom. Since the onset of calculator use, an increasing number of students have become dependent on electronic technologies to solve basic number facts and operations with numbers. Long-term dependence, then, on electronic technologies such as calculators, tablets, or smartphones runs the risk of experiencing reverse constructivism. In other words, people who are dependent on technology to perform mathematical tasks tend to develop ways of knowing that run counter to creative thinking and conceptual understanding, which are active and progressive motifs associated with Piagetian constructivism. While young children in low-income communities do not frequently have access to calculators (let alone other forms of digital technologies), the idea that overutilization of digital tools in mathematics leads to a form of environmental generational amnesia runs parallel to the way children living in poverty are taught in early childhood settings. Unfortunately, children of poor families are often taught in ways that use rote, mechanical methods. Environmental generational amnesia sets in because young children in these environments begin to construe mathematics as a subject only for privileged people and therefore they believe it to be unimportant in their everyday lives.[2]

Recognizing and Appreciating Mathematical Proclivities in Early Childhood

Thus far, attention has focused on the lack of advocacy for young children's education in general and mathematical education in particular. I introduced the detrimental characteristics associated with mathematical thinking in particular that emerge from the early childhood years, specifically reverse constructivism, a term connected with Kahn's coinage of the term environmental generational amnesia. In the remainder of the chapter, focus will be placed on analyses of young children's mathematical strengths and how parents and research-practitioners need to encourage mathematical proclivities in early childhood as a starting point for future mathematical learning. These analyses are based on the use of naturalistic observation methodology as a means of capturing young children's genuine mathematical and spatial propensities that are based on in-depth observations of preschoolers engaged in everyday free play with play blocks.

The "Big Square"

In an earlier publication, I investigated the spatial thinking of two children, Liza and Sam, with the intent to share an everyday example of young children's strong sense of spatial reasoning when constructing a mini-city within a rectangular region made from play blocks (Ness, Farenga, & Garofalo, 2017). Liza and Sam, both approximately 3 years 6 months, attend a preschool with children from both low- and middle-income families. Liza and Sam are eager to build in the block area after snack time. The children's dialogue was captured and analyzed as well. It was fascinating to discover that both children intended, and succeeded, to construct what they called a "big square." The objective for building the "big square" was only a means to an end—they engaged in pretend play after the "big square" was constructed. For our purposes, we examine Liza and Sam's "big square" through their use of invented strategies in emergent geometric thinking as they organize and systematize their conception of "square." Of particular note is the exactitude that Liza and Sam demonstrate during the building process.

The children made the "big square" from blocks as a way to represent a city on the preschool room floor. This city included various locations signified by different blocks. Each of the blocks indicated different locations within the "big square": their homes; a park; a playground; a market; and their preschool. Liza and Sam showed their engagement in the process of paired-associate learning as they constructed their real-life locations (see Figure 2.1).

It is important to learn the extent to which mathematical thinking arises from this account. To begin, while it is true that Liza and Sam's physical interpretation of the "big square" seemed to look more like a non-square rectangle (two opposite sides are longer than their adjacent sides), they recognized that "square" can be categorized as a geometric figure with four sides and four right angles. Indeed, their knowledge of formal terminologies in geometry is not what is essential here. What is important are their invented strategies and how they interpret the geometric shapes in their everyday environment. Second, the children's steadfastness in precision when constructing the "big square," namely that the rectangular construction is enclosed and appears as a four-sided figure with four right angles constructed of blocks that are placed perpendicularly at the corners, is another hallmark of their construction. Liza and Sam used four types of blocks for their rectangle structure: the half-unit, single-unit, double-unit, and quadruple-unit block. One of the children initially put one quadruple-unit block on the floor so that it appears parallel to the wall at a distance equal to about five unit blocks.

It is important to note that Liza and Sam did not begin to build the perpendicular sides but instead placed a second quadruple-unit block parallel with the wall and with the initial quadruple-unit block. The children continued to assemble the blocks by developing the left perpendicular side. To do so, they used a double-unit block and two single-unit blocks.

Liza and Sam knew that they needed to close the gap, so they obtained two half-unit blocks to close it. The last section to be constructed was the right perpendicular side. At this juncture, Liza and Sam were running out of double-unit and single-unit blocks. In order to complete the "square," the two children knew that they needed four half-unit blocks to finish the shape. The important idea here is that the children use different-size blocks on each side of their rectangular structure to construct parallel sides with right angles—indeed, an intellectually advanced and complex concept that, for most parents and teachers, would seem impossible for young children to understand.

Third, from the perspective of mapping, navigation, and location, Liza and Sam were highly precise in terms of specific symbols represented by individual blocks and their referents. Figure 2.1 shows the children's finished construction, which highlights the locations of their respective apartment buildings in two different locations, the location of the preschool, and the location of the playground where they often meet during outdoor play time. Liza and Sam's block representations of their homes, the preschool, and their playground are anchor points in that within each child's concept map, these locations serve as reference points. In other words, the locations are cognitively salient in their minds—locations that are, for these 3.5-year-old children, essential in their everyday lives. Moreover, Liza and Sam identify the blocks touching within the "big square" as "streets" in their "neighborhood." While the spaces on either side of each child's residence (in an east–west direction, or "up–down" direction) appear vacant—that is, without other blocks next to their own residence—in reality, these "empty spaces" are not empty at all; apartment buildings are continuous and adjacent to both buildings along the streets on which Sam and Liza's families reside. But clearly, each of their homes forms the center of their everyday lives and surroundings.

Why is this important? Through their words and actions, Liza and Sam demonstrate an advanced knowledge of geometry. Skeptics might balk at the idea that the children's "square" demonstrates geometric knowledge in that the shape does not have "precisely measured" side lengths and that they created a rectangle from play blocks. These skeptics are perhaps right from a Euclidean perspective. But there is more—namely, that the children's unique thinking strategies suggest the development of cognitive propensities that relate to the unidirectional character of polygonal hierarchy. That is, while Liza and Sam's ordering was inaccurate from a Euclidean perspective, they have sophisticated knowledge of quadrilaterals (i.e., the relationship between rectangles and squares) as they recognize and appreciate the intrinsic relationships of shapes. Moreover, it is important to note two things.

First, at about 3 years 6 months of age, Liza and Sam were engaged in mathematical thinking during free play; they were not taught formally about squares and rectangles. Their use of "square" most likely emanates from listening to adults or older peers use the term in association with a four-sided figure.

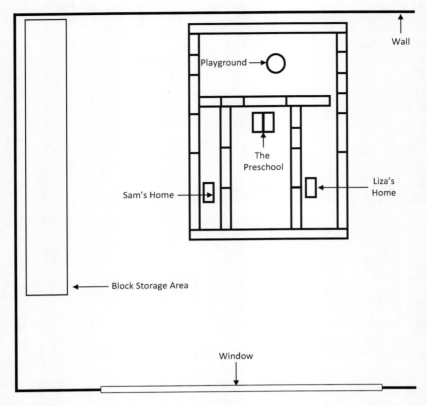

Figure 2.1 Liza and Sam's Play Block Representation of a Big Square.

It would be difficult to imagine their use of the term had they been taught about the concept of square at such a young age. And second, Liza and Sam's geometric ability far exceeds the so-called first level of Dina van Hiele's model for the development of geometric reasoning (van Hiele-Geldof, 1957; Hoffer, 1981). Individuals are identified as Level 0 (i.e., the first level) when they construe basic geometric figures solely through visual means—in other words, without consideration of geometric properties that define specific polygons. Moreover, Sam and Liza's mathematical ideas are not solely based on the identification of shapes. The children are also able to appreciate properties of shapes and connect them with real-life situations. To conclude, it is not important that Liza and Sam refer to a rectangular layout of blocks as a square. What is important is to recognize and value the children's intellectual propensities associated with spatial skills and emergent mathematical ideas. Parents, teachers, administrators, and researchers need to take note that young children's informal geometric skills evident in their mapping and navigation abilities are highly multifaceted and must serve as an important impetus for future learning in school.

Early Childhood Informal Arithmetic

The previous example demonstrated preschool children's adeptness in informal geometric thinking as they contemplated shape and distance. The following dialogue also presents two children, Alex (4 years 7 months) and Ken (4 years 5 months), engaged in constructive free play with blocks. I encourage readers to examine the two children's discourse (below) as they share in block play and, during the course of investigation, to determine the kinds of mathematical thinking in which the children are engaging. As a point of reference, Ken is bringing quadruple blocks (blocks that are four times the length of the common unit block) to a structure that is made of four posts (cylinder blocks) and two beams (quadruple blocks). So, the four posts indicate that the building will have four walls that can either be covered or left open. The two beams make it possible for the children to construct a second floor (see Figure 2.2). Alex is looking on and commenting on what needs to be done to complete the structure. The following dialogue captures the essence of their intuitive and highly complex mathematical thinking:

Alex: Here. One. We need . . . we need two more. Now we need . . . we still need two more.

Ken: We need one more . . .

Alex: Oh! Two more or one more?

Ken: Oh, you were right—two more.

Alex: I was right—two more.

Ken: You was right—two more.
[The two boys complete the second level of their structure, which consists of eight touching quadruple blocks placed adjacently along the longest side.]

Ken: We got to cover these up, right?
[Ken takes another quadruple block for the purpose of covering the sides, which appear as the walls of the square structure.]

Alex: Ken, we're gonna need more [quadruple-sized blocks] to make the house!

Ken: I know! We can cover it! Like that!

Alex: No . . .

Ken: But this is the wall . . . to keep everything inside!

Alex: Okay. We're gonna need . . . [pauses for approximately three seconds] . . . uhm, eight.

Ken: Pick up seven of them [the quadruple-sized blocks. He says "seven" because he took one out to cover one of the sides].

Alex: Okay that's it. Now we're going to put some more right here.

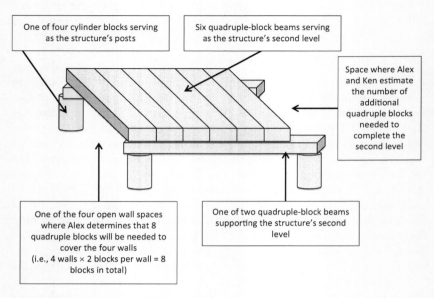

One of four cylinder blocks serving as the structure's posts

Six quadruple-block beams serving as the structure's second level

Space where Alex and Ken estimate the number of additional quadruple blocks needed to complete the second level

One of the four open wall spaces where Alex determines that 8 quadruple blocks will be needed to cover the four walls (i.e., 4 walls × 2 blocks per wall = 8 blocks in total)

One of two quadruple-block beams supporting the structure's second level

Figure 2.2 Alex and Ken's Structure.

Ken and Alex's scenario will be analyzed both in terms of dialogue and actions that are evidenced by the components in Figure 2.2. It should be clear from the start that the children's use of estimation plays an important role in the construction of their block building. Given that Ken and Alex are not the only two children who engage in free play, it is posited, and supported in prior research, that estimation is an emergent cross-cutting mathematical process skill evident in all children's free play activities (Ginsburg, Pappas, & Seo, 2001; McVarish, 2012; Ness & Farenga, 2007; Siegler & Ramani, 2008). While estimation skill is a work in progress in that it tends to develop from a seemingly logarithmic (i.e., exaggerated) psychological representation of numbers to a more linear (i.e., one-to-one correspondent) one (Dehaene, 2011; Siegler & Booth, 2004), estimation can be observed and identified in virtually all young children's everyday, real-life situations. Further, the children used estimation in a way that moved beyond the overestimations of logarithmic representation. In many experimental studies involving estimation, children are asked to engage in placing numerals from 1 to 100 or 1 to 1,000 on a number line—abstractions that are far removed from their everyday activities. Because Alex and Ken were using their imagination in play, their activity in constructing a building made of blocks was not removed from their everyday actions; that is, they were not asked to participate in an arbitrary task that is detached from the everyday goings-on of their environment.

Next, what happens after Ken convinces Alex that they can cover the "walls" with the quadruple blocks? Ken says, "I know! We can cover [the wall]! Like that!" and further convinces Alex by saying, "But this is the wall . . . to keep everything inside!" Alex agrees, and then thinks for a few seconds about how many quadruple blocks will be needed to cover each of the walls. He then gives an astonishing answer: "We're gonna need . . . uhm, eight."

At this point, it is important to ask two questions: First, why does Alex say "eight"? And second, how does he arrive at that conclusion? We might conclude that Alex arrives at "eight" because he is using two mathematical processes to get an answer: estimation and multiplication. He uses estimation again because he is thinking that each wall will need two stacked quadruple blocks in order to be covered. He arrives at his conclusion by conjecturing that if each wall can be covered by two stacked blocks, and there are four walls in total, there must be eight blocks needed in total to cover all four walls. Alex's statement demonstrates a remarkable example of informal multiplication. He is not using the standard algorithm for multiplication that involves abstract symbolism. Rather, he solved this multiplication problem while engaged in free play. Consider also that Ken responds to Alex by saying, "Pick up seven of them [the quadruple-sized blocks]." One can gather from Ken's response that he, too, is multiplying (as well as subtracting); one block was already placed against one of the "walls" of the house. So, if eight blocks are needed in total, then seven more are needed to complete the job.

Readers might question the idea of early childhood multiplication. After all, multiplication is taught in third grade—possibly the end of second—and continues into the upper elementary grade levels. But it is important to consider that young children, and older children too, don't need abstract symbolism to succeed in solving complex mathematical problems. I am not arguing that children should not learn the formal multiplication algorithm; on the contrary, they should learn it when they are ready to do so—especially when they are prepared to connect the concept of repeated addition or base-10 concepts with the abstract formal multiplication symbolism. But this process can only happen if society has an unambiguous, vested interest in young children and their development and dispenses with the unwarranted notion that children's play (and play of older individuals, for that matter) does not influence intellectual development. It absolutely does!

Investing in Young Children's Futures

So how might it be possible to avoid the pitfalls of young children's experiences so that they enjoy mathematics to the extent that they succeed in it and love it for the rest of their lives? Further, how might it be possible to increase the likelihood that all preschool children succeed in their mathematical activities? Below are five ways that these tasks can be accomplished:

1   Parents, teachers, caregivers, and education administrators and policymakers should avoid adopting federal or state-sanctioned programs that are based on unsubstantiated evidence of how young children learn and lean less on unfounded top-down theories of formalization with young children. They instead should focus greater attention on young children's natural, intellectual propensities based on each child's invented strategies in solving problems—nearly all of which are mathematical in content. There is ample evidence both suggesting and demonstrating that uninterrupted free play influences intellectual development in general and mathematical development in particular (Christie & Johnsen, 1983; Ginsburg, 2007; Main, 1983; Ness & Farenga, 2007; Vygotsky, 1933/1966).

2   Mathematics materials should serve to enhance young children's engagement in mathematical thinking, not stifle it. Young children don't need fancy, elaborate manipulatives to learn mathematics (Elkind, 2007). Materials with high levels of affordance (i.e., materials designed for a specific purpose or with elaborate instructions) have been shown to do the opposite of what they were originally set out to do by the developer or manufacturer (Ness & Farenga, 2016). Instead of increasing young children's intellectual propensities, manipulatives with multiple capabilities and uses or those that are scripted through elaborate sets of instructions run the risk of lowering levels of engagement and intellectual fascination and motivation. To this end, there is little, if any, reason for young children to use fancy manipulatives, such as fraction strips or base-10 blocks, in the early childhood setting. Not only will children be less likely to participate in mathematical activities; teachers will more than likely begin teaching with manipulatives as well. All children learn through active engagement. So, free play with blocks or planks (1×3×15 cm wooden cuboids) will be more effective in providing an environment of wonder and fascination in mathematics. In sum, young children—and older children too—need to play in order to engage in mathematical imagination. Thus, educators whose mission is to diminish inequities in early childhood mathematics need to balance the playing field by ensuring that all early childhood settings have the necessary materials that encourage wonder and fascination (McVarish, 2012).

3   Informal assessment should play a minimal, yet supportive role—and formalized assessment should play no role!—in early childhood mathematical experiences. Discovery and invention should play a maximal role if mathematical curriculum occurs in a teaching and learning environment at the preschool level. In this regard, the factors of schooling—curriculum, teaching, and assessment—should be integrated in a way

that fosters and promotes discovery learning experiences (Farenga, Joyce, & Ness, 2002). For example, *Big Math for Little Kids* (Greenes, Ginsburg, & Balfanz, 2004) is one math program for young children that has been demonstrated to be based on corroborated evidence of how children learn. The contents within it have the potential to help all children learn math from experience and what the children themselves exhibit as they invent their own strategies in everyday settings.

4   After-school programs are often one of the few ways, if not the only way, for young children of poor families to engage in enrichment activities in mathematics. The idea here is not to have children write math, fill in worksheets, or to engage in rote, superficial activities. We know from mathematics development research that these activities do much more harm than good (Ginsburg, 1989; Starkey & Klein, 2008). Instead, after-school or after-preschool programs must serve young children by providing favorable environments that foster learning mathematics for its own sake and for the fun of it. Young children, and older children for that matter, don't need to know the names of things and memorize disconnected facts. Rather, they need to be provided settings in which they can engage in activities in which they ask why something happens or how something works out. Teaching math concepts in early childhood settings is fruitless and potentially destructive. Instead, preschools should serve all children, regardless of SES, and function as wellsprings for play, imagination, and informal mathematical and scientific discovery.

5   We need to stop using Orwellian doublespeak, particularly euphemistic terminologies in education and mathematical thinking, to claim how "wonderful" education policy is when it is often a pretense for something more nefarious—namely, diminishing children's success and love of learning, exploration, and discovery. Further, use of such detrimental language has led to increases in nonsensical testing of preschool children as well as those in elementary school and, thus, limitations in play time and opportunities for creativity, imagination, and reflection. For-profit enterprises benefit from the repetitive nature of such terminologies—such as "standards" and "high-stakes assessment"—because school districts capitulate to state policymakers into purchasing instructional and assessment-related publications that focus on the misplaced need for standardized testing. To this end, both parents and educators need to challenge the motives of for-profit corporations as well as their state legislators to determine if they are really on the side of children.

Notes

1 Without operationalizing terms and with minimal to no evidence from research, state and federal lawmakers and educational administrators have implemented rubric assessment to reach an understanding of how to define the ambiguous and elusive term "proficient" in the context of meeting educational standards.

For education lawmakers and administrators, "proficient" appears to mean that a student has achieved a learning objective and has mastered a specific standard or norm. Rubric assessment is oppressive; it sorely limits children's freedoms and future opportunities (Ho, 2008; Pinar, 2017). Moreover, many rubrics that are intended to enhance assessment supply little, if any, additional data to teachers, parents, and policymakers. Rather, rubrics serve as merely semantic enigmas that often include imprecise terminologies for the purpose of misinforming parents and caregivers. Vague terms such as "proficient," "satisfactory," "competent," "needs improvement," "developing," and so forth—terms that have multiple meanings that depend on context—have been used in a one-size-fits-all manner to describe students who are frequently led to believe that their current levels of effort will lead to successful future activities. But evidence suggests that this perception of accomplishment is profoundly misplaced (Farenga, Ness, & Sawyer, 2015).

2 It is important to note that not all children of low-SES families experience environmental generational amnesia—particularly with regard to mathematical thinking. Moreover, it is possible for middle- and upper-SES children to develop the mindset that mathematics is a "privileged" subject that only few people can understand.

References

Brooks-Gunn, J., Duncan, G. J., Klebanov, P. K., & Sealand, N. (1993). Do neighborhoods influence child and adolescent development? *American Journal of Sociology, 99*(2), 353–395.

Chin-Lun Hung, G., Hahn, J., Alamiri, B., Buka, S. L., Goldstein, J. M., Laird, N., Nelson, C. A., Smoller, J. W., & Gilman, S. E. (2015). Socioeconomic disadvantage and neural development from infancy through early childhood. *International Journal of Epidemiology, 44*(6), 1889–1899.

Cho, S. H., Fang, X., Tayur, S., & Xu, Y. (2015). Combating child labor: Incentives and information transparency in global supply chains. Working Paper. Carnegie Mellon University.

Christie, J. F., & Johnsen, E. P. (1983). The role of play in social-intellectual development. *Review of Educational Research, 53*(1), 93–115.

Copley, J. V. (2000). *The young child and mathematics.* Washington, DC: National Association for the Education of Young Children.

Dehaene, S. (2011). *The number sense: How the mind creates mathematics.* New York: Oxford University Press.

DeVries, R., & Zan, B. (1994). *Moral classrooms, moral children: Creating a constructivist atmosphere in early education* (Vol. 47). New York: Teachers College Press.

Diamond, J. (2005). *Collapse: How societies choose to fail or succeed.* New York: Penguin.

Drummond, B., & Steele, S. J. (2017). The Natural Histories Project: Interview with Peter Kahn. Available at: naturalhistoriesproject.org/conversations/environmental-generational-amnesia.

Elkind, D. (2007). *The power of play: How spontaneous, imaginative activities lead to happier, healthier children.* Boston, MA: Da Capo.

Farenga, S. J., & Ness, D. (2007). Making a community information guide about nonpoint source pollution. *Science Scope, 30*(5), 12–14.

Farenga, S. J., Joyce, B. A., & Ness, D. (2002). Reaching the zone of optimal learning: The alignment of curriculum, instruction, and assessment. In R. Bybee

(Ed.), *Learning science and the science of learning* (pp. 51–62). Arlington, VA: NSTA Press.

Farenga, S. J., Ness, D., & Sawyer, R. D. (2015). Avoidance of equivalence by leveling: Challenging the consensus-driven curriculum that defines students as "average." *Journal of Curriculum Theorizing, 30*(3), 8–27.

Ginsburg, H. P. (1989). *Children's arithmetic: How they learn it and how you teach it.* Austin, TX: Pro Ed.

Ginsburg, H. P., & Opper, S. (1988). *Piaget's theory of intellectual development.* Englewood Cliffs, NJ: Prentice-Hall.

Ginsburg, H. P., Pappas, S., & Seo, K. H. (2001). Everyday mathematical knowledge: Asking young children what is developmentally appropriate. In S. Golbeck (Ed.), *Psychological perspectives on early childhood education: Reframing dilemmas in research and practice* (pp. 181–219). Mahwah, NJ: Lawrence Erlbaum Associates.

Ginsburg, K. R. (2007). The importance of play in promoting healthy child development and maintaining strong parent-child bonds. *Pediatrics, 119*(1), 182–191.

Greenes, C. (1999). Ready to learn: Developing young children's mathematical powers. In J. Copley (Ed.), *Mathematics in the early years* (pp. 39–47). Reston, VA: NCTM.

Greenes, C., Ginsburg, H. P., & Balfanz, R. (2004). Big math for little kids. *Early Childhood Research Quarterly, 19*(1), 159–166.

Ho, A. D. (2008). The problem with "proficiency": Limitations of statistics and policy under No Child Left Behind. *Educational Researcher, 37*(6), 351–360.

Hoffer, A. (1981). Geometry is more than proof. *Mathematics Teacher, 74*, 11–18.

Johnson, D. D., & Johnson, B. (2006). *High stakes: Poverty, testing, and failure in American schools.* Lanham, MD: Rowman & Littlefield.

Johnson, D. D., Johnson, B., Farenga, S. J., & Ness, D. (2008). *Stop high-stakes testing: An appeal to America's conscience.* Lanham, MD: Rowman & Littlefield.

Kahn, P. H. (2002). Children's affiliations with nature: Structure, development, and the problem of environmental generational amnesia. In P. H. Kahn & S. R. Kellert (Eds.), *Children and nature: Psychological, sociocultural, and evolutionary investigations* (pp. 93–116). Cambridge, MA: MIT Press.

Kahn, P. H. (2011). *Technological nature: Adaptation and the future of human life.* Cambridge, MA: MIT Press.

Leventhal, T., & Brooks-Gunn, J. (2000). The neighborhoods they live in: The effects of neighborhood residence on child and adolescent outcomes. *Psychological Bulletin, 126*(2), 309.

Main, M. (1983). Exploration, play, and cognitive functioning related to infant-mother attachment. *Infant Behavior and Development, 6*(2–3), 167–174.

Mariani, M. (2017, July 3). How income inequality is messing with kids' brains: Inside the nationwide study exploring the link between poverty and brain development. *Mother Jones.* Available at: www.motherjones.com/politics/2017/07/neuroscience-poverty-brains-trump-clinton.

McVarish, J. (2012). *Where's the wonder in elementary math?: Encouraging mathematical reasoning in the classroom.* New York: Routledge.

Ness, D., & Farenga, S. J. (2007). *Knowledge under construction: The importance of play in developing children's spatial and geometric thinking.* Lanham, MD: Rowman & Littlefield.

Ness, D., & Farenga, S. J. (2016). Blocks, bricks, and planks: Relationships between affordance and visuo-spatial constructive play objects. *American Journal of Play, 8*(2), 201–227.

Ness, D., Farenga, S. J., & Garofalo, S. G. (2017). *Spatial intelligence: Why it matters from birth through adolescence.* New York: Routledge.

Newcombe, N. S. (2011). What is neoconstructivism? *Child Development Perspectives,* 5(3), 157–160.

Noble, K. G., Norman, M. F., & Farah, M. J. (2005). Neurocognitive correlates of socioeconomic status in kindergarten children. *Developmental Science,* 8(1), 74–87.

Noble, K. G., Houston, S. M., Brito, N. H., Bartsch, H., Kan, E., Kuperman, J. M., et al. (2015). Family income, parental education and brain structure in children and adolescents. *Nature Neuroscience,* 18(5), 773–778.

Parker, D. (2007). *Before their time: The world of child labor.* New York: Quantuck Lane Press.

Piaget, J. (1954). *The construction of reality in the child.* New York: Basic Books.

Pinar, W. F. (2017). The sadism of school reform. In D. Ness & S. J. Farenga (Eds.), *Alternatives to privatizing public education and curriculum: Festschrift in honor of Dale D. Johnson* (pp. 3–17). New York: Routledge.

Ravitch, D. (2013). *Reign of error: The hoax of the privatization movement and the danger to America's public schools.* New York: Vintage.

Seo, K. H., & Ginsburg, H. P. (2004). What is developmentally appropriate in early childhood mathematics education? Lessons from new research. In D. H. Clements & J. Sarama (Eds.), *Engaging young children in mathematics: Standards for early childhood mathematics education* (pp. 91–104). Mahwah, NJ: Lawrence Erlbaum Associates.

Siegler, R. S., & Booth, J. L. (2004). Development of numerical estimation in young children. *Child Development,* 75(2), 428–444.

Siegler, R. S., & Ramani, G. B. (2008). Playing linear numerical board games promotes low-income children's numerical development. *Developmental Science,* 11(5), 655–661.

Smith, W. C. (2016). An introduction to the global testing culture. In W. C. Smith (Ed.), *The global testing culture: Shaping education policy, perceptions, and practice* (pp. 7–24). Oxford, UK: Symposium Books Ltd.

Starkey, P., & Klein, A. (2008). Sociocultural influences on young children's mathematical knowledge. In O. N. Saracho & B. Spodek (Eds.), *Contemporary perspectives on mathematics in early childhood education* (pp. 253–276). Charlotte, NC: Information Age Publishing.

UNICEF. (2016). *Ending extreme poverty: A focus on children.* Washington, DC: UNICEF.

van Hiele-Geldof, D. (1957). *"De Didaktiek van de meetkunde in de eerste klas van het VHMO": The didactics of geometry in the lowest class of the secondary school.* University of Utrecht: Doctoral dissertation.

Vygotsky, L. (1933/1966). Play and its role in the psychological development of the child. Lecture, Leningrad Pedagogical Institute. *Problems of Psychology,* 6, 62–76.

Wessells, M. (2009). *Child soldiers: From violence to protection.* Cambridge, MA: Harvard University Press.

3   Literacy

Poverty, Literacy, and the American Dream: Do Children Fail in Schools, or Do Society and Schools Fail Children?

Michael R. Sampson

Introduction

Why do many poor young children fail to become readers in the primary schools of America? How serious is this problem that keeps children and families in a generational cycle of poverty and illiteracy? What are the causes of illiteracy? And finally, what can be done to break this cycle? In this chapter, I will discuss poverty in the United States and the special stresses it places on young children and their learning to read. I will examine what the government has done to help, and then turn to a discussion of best practices of teaching reading to children in poor and urban settings.

Poverty and Hunger

As a young idealistic professor, I was able to lead as chair in a university partnership that connected my university faculty and student teachers to the most poverty-stricken areas of Dallas, Texas (Stetson et al., 2001). We brought to the partnership expertise in how children learn and provided literacy interactive strategies that we passed on to teachers via professional development. But I was the one who had the most to learn. City Park Elementary School was located in the canyon area of Dallas, where highways connected Dallasites passing over the concrete canyon to the places they worked. Below the overpasses, homeless people attempted to survive through public assistance and begging. And they had children, and those children were in my partnership school. Many of these children lived in homeless shelters. The majority had only one parent, and virtually all of the pupils came to school hungry. I was struck by the dull, lifeless eyes of these 5-year-olds and my failure to engage them in literacy strategies that had worked for me in other settings. Our program succeeded and was nationally recognized as the best teacher education program in the nation (American Association of State Colleges and Universities [AASCU], 2017), but the asterisk that always will burn in my heart is our failure to make a true difference at City Park Elementary School. We were able to bring the resources of people and plans—with great professional development and faculty and teacher residents eager to make a difference. But we were not able to bring food and shelter and a sense of wellbeing, which were their greatest needs. Maslow defined this for us in the last century with his Hierarchy of Needs (Maslow, 1943). Children must have safety, security, and food if they are to learn. Without this baseline of physiological and safety needs, school achievement will be difficult.

In the thirty years since that experience, have we turned the corner on poverty? The answer is no; the statistics continue the sad story.

The National Center for Children in Poverty (2017) reports that almost one in four American children live in poverty as defined by the federal poverty threshold. They cite research, however, that shows this threshold is too low, and that 46% of children actually live in low-income families, where they struggle with enough money for food and housing and clothing, as well as access to medical services. This translates to classrooms where teachers are teaching to children that are hungry. And as referenced above in Maslow's research, learning occurs best when physiological needs have been met.

Can Government Help? Politics and Literacy

We do not have to make the argument that literacy is important and that young children need to learn to read. From the President of the United States to the governors of states, the message has been consistent: Reading is important. Consider these words from Barack Obama (2005) when he was in office:

> I believe that if we want to give our children the best possible chance in life, if we want to open doors of opportunity while they're young and teach them the skills they'll need to succeed later on, then one of our greatest responsibilities as citizens, as educators, and as parents is to ensure that every American child can read and read well. Reading is the gateway skill that makes all other learning possible, from complex word problems and the meaning of our history to scientific discovery and technological proficiency. In a knowledge economy where this kind of learning is necessary for survival, how can we send our kids out into the world if they're only reading at a fourth-grade level?

History has proven, though, that government "help" is not effective in increasing literacy success of children living in poverty. From President Reagan to President Obama, increased government spending has done little to increase the success of creating a nation of readers. Below is a timeline of government intervention into the policies and practices of states and local schools.

President Ronald Reagan believed that the poor achievement of American school children was a threat to national security. Under the leadership of his Secretary of Education Terrell Bell, the federal government created a blue-ribbon panel on the state of education in the United States. Their report, "A Nation at Risk" (U.S. Department of Education, 1983), was very critical of the American education system. Unfortunately, the report started the trend toward more standardized testing and less trust of teachers. I believe that the resulting practice of "teaching to the test" has actually done more harm to schools and student achievement than helped.

President Bill Clinton supported greater professional development in reading education for teachers. His plan, "Goals 2000: Educate America Act" (U.S. Department of Education, 1994), was intended to raise literacy achievement through better teaching; however, he also required the implementation of a nationwide testing program in reading and mathematics to measure national progress toward goals. Schools were required to do even more testing.

President George W. Bush, in 2001, followed Clinton and the trend toward national interference in state education policy and practice by signing the controversial bill and act entitled "No Child Left Behind" (NCLB). Within this legislation, federal money favored purchasing products developed by publishers to teach phonics over the successful teacher-led practice of teaching reading through reading books. But an even greater flaw of NCLB was more requirements for standardized tests. Such tests are even more damaging to children at risk in urban areas, as they contain cultural and linguistic biases, including testing recently immigrated non-English-speaking students in a foreign language—English. So instead of schools being able to teach young children how to read, they were forced to spend most of the academic year preparing for the tests that would come in the spring. Such tests usually indicated that the students were failing, largely because they were being compared to upper-middle-class students from other parts of the country, and because for many, the tests were given in a new language they were in the process of learning.

President Barack Obama came into office with the good intentions of improving the literacy achievement of children and seeing these improvements as a pathway to solving personal, social, and economic problems of urban families. His signature legislation was passed in pursuit of these goals (United States Department of Education, 2010). He unfortunately listened to the wrong advisors, and his education department was no better than those of the failures of past presidents. Even the name of his 4.3-billion-dollar program, "Race to the Top," was flawed. Learning is not a race—with winners and losers—rather, it is a process where everyone learns and all states and schools and children can be winners. Instead, states were asked to submit grant requests to receive federal funds, and some were winners and some were losers. Access to federal funding should be based on need, not competition. In reality, the real winners may have been those states not awarded the funds. "Race to the Top" required that teachers be evaluated and rewarded in relation to their students' test scores. This concept is flawed because it makes standardized tests on basic, low-level skills more important than ever, leading teachers to be even more focused on raising test scores. Good teaching is not about achieving high test scores; rather, it's about reaching children and teaching to the whole child. Further, as discussed in this chapter, we need our very best teachers in urban schools with high poverty. "Race to the Top" is driving our best teachers to the suburbs, where students tend to score higher on standardized tests (because of opportunities funded by well-off families), thus giving teachers higher ratings and salaries.

In summary, the federal government with their well-intentioned but flawed educational reforms is doing more to hinder than to help urban schools and children in poverty. A better solution would be to send tax money back to the local schools and districts for use to truly help children in need, and to empower teachers to teach children without federally required mandates and programs. And finally, standardized tests should not be required, or at least be delayed until students reach high school.

Learning

School breakfast and school lunch programs are helping, but once those needs are partially met and we move to curriculum and school instruction, what is key? Or what really matters?

The teacher matters the most. I base this statement on the findings of the classical First Grade Studies from the 1960s. This research (Bond & Dykstra, 1967) attempted to determine which instructional approach to teaching reading worked best. The results were confusing—sometimes Language Experience classrooms were most effective. In other classrooms, ITA, or Initial Teaching Alphabet, was superior. In discussing these mixed findings, Bond and Dykstra (1967) mused, "Evidently, reading achievement is influenced by factors peculiar to school systems over and above differences in pre-reading capabilities" (pp. 121–122). In the years that followed, the studies came to be remembered by one truth that signified success in all approaches—the key was the teacher, and the adage became "the teacher makes the difference."

The Importance of School/University Partnerships: It Takes a Village to Train a Teacher

Taking the conclusions of the First Grade Studies one step further and their finding that the teacher makes the difference, what's key in teacher education is creating good teachers. In order to do so, I used the framework of the City Park Elementary School award-winning program I referenced earlier and implemented it in New York City. This was in partnership with the New York City Department of Education, the largest school district in the United States with more than 1.1 million students (American Association of Colleges of Teacher Education, 2017). We named the program RISE—

Residential Internship for St. John's Educators. In highlighting the essence of the program to AACTE, I shared:

> The RISE program was created in partnership with the New York City public schools to provide our students a clinically rich, 1-year student teaching program. By imbedding our faculty and residents into the public schools, we are preparing teachers who are ready to teach on Day 1 of their first teaching job. They have experienced a full year of school under the coaching of their school mentor and St. John's faculty member and understand the culture of schools and the demands teachers encounter. RISE has transformed not only our residents, but our faculty as well.

If "the teacher makes the difference," and I believe that the teacher does, we wanted to create a program that trains teachers, in an urban setting rich with diversity, to be outstanding educators. The partnership worked both ways—we provided student residents to the schools in a one-year resident program, and they provided access to their schools to our faculty and students. We sought the input of the school leadership and teachers on our course outlines and rubrics, and we gave back to them through on-school-site professional development.

School/university partnerships are important because future teachers are trained in the context and practice of real schools. In addition to the obstacles excellent teacher education programs face when they operate in poor urban areas with child hunger, there is also a threat from school curriculum that is artificial or scripted. Research indicates that teachers that know sound strategies have difficulty transferring them into teaching when the curriculum is dictated and the teacher becomes a robot following an external script (Sampson, Linek, Raine, & Szabo, 2013). School leadership has a vital role in clearing scripted programs and freeing teachers to become artists and creators of interactive learning environments in their classrooms. The best scenario and results occur when good teachers teach in programs that allow them to be creative and student focused.

Best Curriculum for Children in Poverty

All children deserve quality schools that are staffed with well-trained, compassionate teachers, and a curriculum that is interactive and thought provoking. Inner-city schools often have the least prepared teachers and a scripted curriculum that would be boring and difficult to comprehend even by the most advantaged students. Thus, our poorest children and their at-risk families often receive the poorest education possible. Jonathan Kozol (1991) writes about this mismatch between the haves and the have-nots, and terms it "savage inequalities." I have already written about our efforts to provide urban schools with high-quality teachers. I now turn to a discussion of the best literacy curriculum for young students, with examples.

Predictable Books

Perhaps no one has made more contributions to helping young children become literate than Bill Martin, Jr. (Sampson, 2014). Martin's passion for helping children of poverty learn to read emanated from his own experience of growing up poor in rural Kansas in the 1920s. Like many children from his small town, the public schools failed him, and he finished school almost illiterate. But a teacher appeared in his life that helped him make the connections between language, speech, writing, and reading. Martin himself became a teacher, a principal, a children's book author, and the principal leader of a theoretical framework of literacy called Sounds of Language, as defined by his Instant Readers and the classic test *Brown Bear, Brown Bear, What Do You See?* (Martin, 1967). Martin was elected to the Reading Hall of Fame and was selected by the International Reading Association as one of the Greats of the 20th Century. His philosophy of reading has special appeal to teachers of at-risk populations who are living in poverty or for children with special needs.

Simply expressed, Martin believed that reading was more in the reader than on the page. He learned in his early days as an elementary school principal that the key to learning to read was to connect the language children loved to the books they read. Language that came in through the ear of the child could be read through the eyes of the child when that language was catchy and memorable.

Martin captured such language in the books he wrote, and young children, even in preschool or kindergarten, regardless of socioeconomic status, successfully read his books. These books incorporated various linguistic elements to make the text accessible to the child. Some books, such as *Brown Bear*, can be read on the first day. Others take a few more days, but quickly become independent reading for the young child.

Predictable books feature rhyming patterns that enable young children to read aloud as they predict the language on the page. Reading begins through the ears and through the eyes as children hear the melody of language and see the beauty of the picture book art. The key is not to rush the child, but to realize that with each repeated reading, the child is depositing the literary structure and sentence patterns in his or her linguistic storehouse.

Brown Bear is an example of a predictable book. Predictability comes from the inclusion of rhyme, rhythm, and repetition of phrases or sentences in the text. A bear is asked what it sees, the bear responds with a rhyme that refers to another animal, that animal is asked what it sees, it responds with a rhyme that refers to a different animal, and so on, until the story ends with the children's classroom teacher who responds in rhyme to a final question. Animals of various colors are used in the book, and long vowel *e* word-family members are used in the questions and rhyming responses. Virtually all children can "read" the text using the picture cues and memory of the predictable stanzas. And with success comes enjoyment and pride.

But how does a child move from being read the book to reading it independently? The answer? The same way they learn to talk from listening and interacting with other language users. In learning to read, children begin the process through inputting language through the ear. Reading has its beginning behind the eye, in the brain, and not in front of the eyes (Smith, 1979). Later, after they have internalized language and stories, they begin to equate what is in the mind to what is on the page. As they read these phrases and words, they realize that letters, sounds, and patterns of letters are repeated in words, and the child begins to internalize phonics. This knowledge is then applied to new words, and the child soon bursts into independent reading.

Our research (Sampson, Briggs, & Sampson, 1986) has shown that young children are more successful reading and comprehending predictable books than any other type of curriculum material, including basal readers. Thus, it's important that children be provided with quality books and a literacy program that has these books as its foundation.

The Language Experience Approach

Another research-based method to help children understand reading is through the Language Experience Approach (LEA). Allen (1999) developed the approach in South Texas and Southern California as a way of having his mostly Spanish-speaking children connect their home language with "book language." Teachers share with students that reading is not hard or difficult—that it's simply "talk written down."

Children are shown that: 1) what I can think about I can talk about, 2) what I talk about can be written down (dictation), and 3) what is written down that I said can be read by me and by others. In the classroom, teachers write down the stories children tell, both one-on-one and in small-group sessions. As the teacher takes dictation, she talks to herself, not teaching directly but reminding herself in audible sound what the students will hear:

I am using alphabet symbols that have names;

Some of the words use capitals for the first letter;

The same letters are used over and over as first letters in words;

Some words appear again and again;

Some ending sounds tell how many and when.

The teacher next reads what has been written and checks it with the student who said it. If it is appropriate, she asks the student to read it with her. Words that appear five or more times are collected for a chart, "Words We

All Use." This chart becomes a major resource for spelling as children begin to write their own stories.

While this seems simple, researchers have noted that dictation provides and demonstrates an important link between thought, language, writing, and reading for students (Cramer, 2001; Sampson & Sampson, 2001). Also, dictation allows the teachers to reinforce the meaning and importance of writing, to offer alternatives to grammar, to demonstrate standard spelling, and to encourage more details to improve the stories.

As teachers, we model reading by reading to children because we want them to want to read. In the same manner, we model writing by writing down what children have to say because we want them to write. We support the child when we take dictation; we enhance their self-esteem as we accept their language and contributions to individual or group efforts. Furthermore, some economically poor children have not had many opportunities to write or scribble at home and really do not understand or value writing. In school, they see their language valued through dictation and grow the confidence to write something down themselves.

When children read stories that they have dictated, comprehension is guaranteed because the stories come from the students, not from authors who are not present. Many teachers use student stories to "publish" student-authored books that are then placed into the class library.

Conclusion

The title of this chapter was coined before I started the research and writing process. I must say that the findings were a disappointment to me. American families that are poor continue to be caught in a cycle of poverty that is very difficult to escape. Despite our efforts for social justice and advocating for children, almost half of the children in the United States are poor today. And with poverty comes a red badge that warns of failure to achieve in the poor schools that urban children tend to attend. I traced Department of Education intervention on states and schools from Reagan to Obama, and concluded that the billions of federal dollars spent had done more harm than good for urban schools. On a brighter side, we are producing better-prepared teachers than ever before, and it is true that the teacher is the most important factor in learning. But they too often face the challenges of teaching children who are hungry and in schools with scripted, low-level instructional programs. To counter this, I have shared two instructional models that are excellent for fostering literacy growth for children.

The American Dream? It remains but continues to be but a dream for poor children in inner cities. But let's not blame the children and the schools for this failure. Instead, let us look at ourselves and ask the question, "What can I do for the poor children of America and for the schools they attend?"

Let us feed the children. Let us feed them with healthy food, and feed them with innovative programs led by outstanding teachers and in schools led by first-class school leaders. When these things occur, I believe our results will change, and the cycle of poverty may be broken.

References

Allen, R. V. (1999). Using Language Experience in beginning reading: How a Language Experience program works. In O. Nelson & W. Linek (Eds.), *Practical classroom applications of Language Experience*. Boston, MA: Allyn & Bacon.

American Association of Colleges of Education. (2017, May). Research-to-practice spotlight turns to RISE at St. John's University. Retrieved from http://edprepmatters.net/2017/05/research-to-practice-spotlight-turns-to-rise-at-st-johns-university.

American Association of State Colleges and Universities (AASCU). (2017, November). Christa McAuliffe Excellence in Teacher Education Award. Retrieved from www.aascu.org/programs/TeacherEd/CMA.

Bond, G. L., & Dykstra, R. (1967). The cooperative research program in first-grade reading instruction. *Reading Research Quarterly*, *2*(4), 5–142.

Cramer, R. L. (2001). *Creative power: The nature and nurture of children's writing*. New York: Longman.

Kozol, J. (1991). *Savage inequalities: Children in America's schools*. New York: Crown Publishing.

Martin, B. (1967). *Brown bear, brown bear, what do you see?* New York: Holt, Rinehart & Winston.

Maslow, A. H. (1943). A theory of human motivation. *Psychological Review*, *50*(4), 370–396.

National Center for Children in Poverty. (2017). Child poverty. Retrieved from www.nccp.org/topics/childpoverty.html.

Obama, B. (2005). Literacy and education in a 21st-century economy. Retrieved from http://obamaspeeches.com/024-Literacy-and-Education-in-a-21st-Century-Economy-Obama-Speech.htm.

Sampson, M. R. (2014). Learning to read naturally: The Martin model of reading. *Childhood Education International: Early Years*, 1–2.

Sampson, M. R., & Sampson, M. B. (2001). The Language Experience approach. Paper presented at the Louisville, KY conference on the International Institute of Literacy Learning.

Sampson, M. R., Briggs, L. D., & Sampson, M. B. (1986). Language, children, and text: Match or mismatch? In M. R. Sampson (Ed.), *The pursuit of literacy: Early reading and writing* (pp. 97–103). Dubuque, IA: Kendall/Hunt Publishing Company.

Sampson, M., Linek, W., Raine, L., & Szabo, S. (2013). The influence of prior knowledge, university coursework, and field experience on primary preservice teachers' use of reading comprehension strategies in a year-long, field-based teacher education program. *Literacy Research and Instruction*, *52*(4), 281–311.

Smith, R. (1979). *Reading without nonsense*. New York: Teachers College Press.

Stetson, E. G., & Stetson, M. R. (1997). Overhauling teacher education: It takes a collaborative. *Education*, *117*(4), 487–495.

Stetson, E., Sandefur, S., Moore, L., Anderson, K., Foote, M., Weaver, S., & Vaughan, J. (2001). To form a more perfect union: How a university and a public school district collaborated to create a field-based master's degree program in elementary education. *Action in Teacher Education*, *17*(2), 58–63.

United States Department of Education. (1983). *A nation at risk: The imperative for educational reform.* A report to the Nation and the Secretary of Education, United States Department of Education. Washington, D.C. Supt. of Docs., U.S. G.P.O. distributor.

United States Department of Education. (1994). *Goals 2000: Educate America Act.* Retrieved from www.tecweb.org/eddevel/telecon/de99.html.

United States Department of Education. (2010). H.R. 6244—111th Congress: Race to the Top Act of 2010. Retrieved from www.govtrack.us/congress/bills/111/hr6244.

4 Physical Sciences

Pediatric Medical Conditions Associated with Poverty

Caitlin Stehling and Robert A. Mangione

Introduction

It has long been recognized that poor children living in the United States are not as healthy as non-poor American children (Brooks-Gunn & Duncan, 1997). Although the disorders selected for discussion in this chapter tend to be more common in poor children, researchers have noted that the relationship between income, income inequality, and disease is very complex. Individuals who serve children, therefore, must recognize that the population of children living in poverty is not homogeneous, which adds to the challenge of applying outcome data to a specific group of youngsters (Nicholas, 2016; Racine, 2016). Those who work directly with children should always consider the specific characteristics of the community they serve and the complexity of its population when assessing what health disorders may be most common in their economically disadvantaged youth. Although school absenteeism is always a concern when confronting health disorders, the impact that medical conditions and their treatments may have upon school readiness, classroom behavior, learning potential, and overall school performance also must be considered.

Medical Conditions Associated with Poverty

Asthma

Asthma is a chronic condition associated with airway inflammation, airway constriction, and increased mucus production resulting in difficulty breathing (Link, 2014). Asthma is characterized by reversible episodes of airway inflammation and constriction, usually due to patient triggers. Common asthma triggers include secondhand smoke, pets, dust mites, air pollution, and cold air. Symptoms of asthma include difficulty breathing, coughing, and wheezing. Asthma in children is one of the most common conditions associated with lower-income children, as well as specific ethnicities. For example, pediatric asthma has higher rates of occurrence in patients of black or African descent (Silber et al., 2017; Barnes, Grant, Hansel, Gao, & Dunston, 2007; Center for Disease Control and Prevention, 2017i; Ciaccio et al., 2014).

Although asthma cannot be cured, it can be managed with medications and trigger avoidance. Asthma medications are broken down into two main categories: rescue medications and maintenance medications. Rescue medications, such as albuterol inhalers, are used to help open the airways and provide immediate relief of asthma symptoms. Maintenance medications may include other types of inhalers or oral medications to help control asthma symptoms long-term and prevent exacerbations. While proper use of maintenance medications has shown a reduction in hospitalizations, they can be considerably more expensive and require more frequent follow-up with a doctor. For example, for a patient without insurance or with limited insurance, commonly used inhalers may cost in excess of $60 per inhaler (Lexicomp®, 2017)—a considerable expenditure when there are few dollars for groceries, rent, utilities, and other expenses.

Albuterol inhalers come in multiple brand names including ProAir®, Ventolin®, and Proventil® (Lexicomp®, 2017). While the inhaler containers may be different colors, all have the same active component of albuterol. Depending on the children's type of asthma, they may need to take their albuterol inhaler before exercise such as a physical education class or recess, as well as when they feel short of breath. Most albuterol inhalers are given on an as-needed basis, every four to six hours. It is essential for educators to be told by health personnel that albuterol inhalers can cause excitement or hyperactivity after use. If students feel as if they are still having trouble breathing after using their albuterol inhaler, it is important that they see the school nurse (if there is one present), or go to the emergency room, as they may be having an asthma attack. Most albuterol inhalers are metered dose inhalers, which means they deliver a set amount of medication directly to the lungs through a short, aerosolized burst. This technique can be difficult for young children to perform, so most physicians recommend the use of a spacer device with the albuterol and certain maintenance inhalers. The spacer device is a cylindrical tube with a face mask or mouthpiece, which is then attached to the inhaler. It helps children receive the full dose of their medications by acting as a holding chamber for the albuterol, where they can use the face mask and breathe normally to receive the full dose of medication (Link, 2014; Potter, 2010; Courtney, McCarter, & Pollart, 2005).

Children with asthma may have asthma exacerbations; episodes where asthma symptoms get progressively worse. When a child has an asthma exacerbation, it often requires a visit to the doctor's office and treatment with oral steroids. During this time, a child may overuse a rescue albuterol inhaler with the hopes of symptom improvement. Tachyphylaxis, or a decreased response due to successive doses of a drug in a short period of time, may occur with albuterol inhaler overuse (Lexicomp®, 2017). Without proper access to preventive and follow-up care, asthma exacerbations may worsen to the point where the child needs inpatient hospitalization for treatment. Children living in poverty or low-income families may not be able to afford medications that would allow their exacerbation to be treated in an outpatient setting (Pacheco et al., 2014).

Other Conditions Associated with Asthma

Allergic Rhinitis

Asthma is also associated with other conditions, including allergic rhinitis and atopic dermatitis. Sometimes children will have all three conditions. Allergic rhinitis, more often known as seasonal allergies, is caused by exposure to allergens in the air, which leads to inflammation of the nasal passages. Signs and symptoms of allergic rhinitis include stuffy or runny nose, sneezing, and red, watery, or itchy eyes. Most signs and symptoms of allergic rhinitis in children may be managed with an over-the-counter, oral antihistamine medication. Over-the-counter medications refer to medications that can be bought at a pharmacy or drugstore without a prescription. Examples of antihistamine medications include cetirizine (Zyrtec®), fexofenadine (Allegra®), loratadine (Claritin®), and diphenhydramine (Benadryl®) (Lexicomp®, 2017). While these medications are safe to use on a daily or seasonal basis, people may experience different levels of sedation with their use. Although cetirizine, fexofenadine, and loratadine are considered non-sedating antihistamines, they may cause some drowsiness with the first few doses of the medication. With daily use, this drowsiness should resolve. Diphenhydramine is considered a sedating antihistamine, and most people may experience severe drowsiness with its use. However, some children may experience a paradoxical reaction, in which they experience hyperactivity instead of sedation. Either the sedation or hyperactivity side effect could potentially impact school behavior or learning. These medications may be given at night to help reduce this side effect. Asthma and allergic rhinitis share some of the same triggers including pets, dust mites, and outdoor allergens (American College of Allergy, Asthma, and Immunology, 2014; Brozek et al., 2017; Mahr & Sheth, 2005; Crystal-Peters, Neslusan, Crown, & Torres, 2002).

Atopic Dermatitis

Atopic dermatitis, also known as eczema, is a medical condition in which patches of dry skin become inflamed, itchy, or red. Sometimes eczema breakouts are the result of exposure to an environmental allergen, but most often eczema has no identifiable cause. Most eczema breakouts can be treated with topical steroid creams or ointments. For those who cannot afford these medications, some patients have success with using moisturizing lotion daily to treat the dry skin and prevent future breakouts. However, severe episodes of eczema which are left untreated may lead to more serious dermatologic complications such as cellulitis or impetigo. Cellulitis is inflammation of the skin tissues, which can rapidly spread. Impetigo is a bacterial skin condition that causes crusty sores on the skin, which are contagious (Lyons, Milner, & Stone, 2015; Eichengield et al., 2015; Tollefson & Bruckner, 2014). Teachers who work in underfunded schools are no strangers to skin problems due to environmental allergens (see Johnson & Johnson, 2006).

Anaphylactic Reactions

Although not specifically associated with poverty, it is important that individuals teaching children from all economic categories recognize that some patients may have more serious allergies, which may require the use of an epinephrine auto-injector, such as EpiPen®. If a child is experiencing an anaphylactic reaction, where they have trouble breathing, the use of an epinephrine auto-injector is recommended. After epinephrine is injected, it is important that children receive immediate medical care (Lexicomp®, 2017). In 2016, the price of EpiPen® had increased from $104 in 2009 to more than $608 in 2016. The price gouging of EpiPen® led to a congressional investigation and legal charges, and the price has since decreased dramatically (CBS News, 2017).

Nutrition-Related Disorders

Malnutrition

Malnutrition refers to lack of proper nutrition or deficiencies in required nutrients. According to the World Health Organization (WHO) (2017b), malnutrition is part of the vicious cycle which includes poverty and disease. Malnutrition causes an imbalance between the body's supply of energy and the body's demand for energy use to enable proper growth and function. This imbalance can be caused by either inadequate intake resulting in underweight patients with wasting and growth stunting, or excessive energy intake causing overweight or obese patients. Individuals who are malnourished are at a higher risk of infection. Malnutrition may cause other deficiencies such as iron, protein, vitamins A or C, or iodine deficiency. Pediatric malnutrition is caused by numerous factors including insufficient food intake, poor food quality, and infection or disease exposure. These conditions are worsened when patients lack access to food, housing, and healthcare (WHO, 2017a; Council on Community Pediatrics, 2016).

In addition to stunted growth, poor nutrition in early childhood can lead to impaired cognitive function; both can be irreversible. Other complications of malnutrition include various types of anemia, caused by lack of iron or vitamin B12, often resulting in increased fatigue. Low vitamin D and calcium levels could result in increased risk of fractures (WHO, 2017c).

Obesity

People who are overweight or obese are at increased risk of metabolic complications such as high cholesterol levels, high blood pressure, and type 2 diabetes as they grow older. Although medications may be used in some severe cases in older adolescents, the mainstay of treatment is nonpharmacologic. A healthy lifestyle with daily exercise is recommended, as well as the importance of teaching about healthy food options (Centers for Disease Control and Prevention (CDC), 2017c, 2017j; Levine, 2011; Rogers et al., 2015). In low-income families, however, the regular purchase of foods such as whole grains and fresh fruits and vegetables is too costly a practice.

Diabetes

For children with type 1 diabetes, insulin is required for disease management. Lack of insulin can result in complications such as diabetic ketoacidosis, a condition where the blood sugar levels are extremely high, which can be fatal if untreated. On the other hand, children with type 1 diabetes may also experience hypoglycemia, where they have low levels of blood sugar in the body. This can be even more dangerous than having high levels. It is important for children with diabetes to be able to recognize the signs and symptoms of hypoglycemia and how to self-treat this condition. Signs and symptoms include fast heart rate, sweating, shaking, chills, dizziness, headache, hunger, and confusion. If a child with diabetes experiences hypoglycemia, they need to ingest sugar immediately to help raise their blood sugar. Examples of appropriate options would be orange juice, non-diet soda, or glucose tablets. In addition, it is possible to accidentally overdose on insulin, which could also cause hypoglycemia. While type 1 diabetes is not more common in low-income individuals, these individuals are at a higher risk of complications due to inadequate healthcare access (Dileepan & Feldt, 2013; Gregory, Moore, & Simmons, 2013).

Mental Health Disorders

ADHD

Children who live in poverty are at a higher risk of having a mental health disorder, including attention deficit hyperactivity disorder (ADHD), anxiety, or depression. In addition, children with ADHD are often untreated, which can lead to more serious complications. ADHD has the highest rates in boys and poor white children. The CDC conducted a survey of parents that showed 11% of children aged four to 17 years were diagnosed with ADHD. This disorder can lead to lack of focus, impulsivity, or disruptions in the classroom (*ChildTrends DataBank*, 2014; CDC, 2017a; Pulcini, Zima, Kelleher, & Houtrow, 2017; Russell, Ford, & Russell, 2015).

The most common class of medications used to treat ADHD are stimulants such as amphetamine salts (Adderall®) and methylphenidate (Ritalin®) (Lexicomp®, 2017). Of note, stimulants are classified as controlled medications per federal pharmacy law. This requires more stringent requirements for the prescriber physician, as well as the family. Most pediatricians require extensive paperwork to be completed by the child's family and child's teachers or psychiatry consults before prescribing. With these restrictions, it can be difficult to obtain these medications even for children who do have insurance. For children without insurance, it is even more challenging. Multiple formulations of stimulants are available in generic form; however, they are often too expensive to purchase out-of-pocket for low-income families. Common side effects of stimulant medications include appetite suppression and insomnia. After the effects of these medications wear off, children may experience *hangry* episodes. *Hangry* (a combination of the words *hungry* and *angry*) is a relatively new term that describes irritability as a result of hunger. Many children with ADHD may become hangry after their medicine wears off because their appetite was suppressed during the day due to a side effect from their ADHD medication. The time at which children might experience hangriness is dependent on which medication they receive, as they have different durations. An alternative class of medications used to treat ADHD are nonstimulants such as guanfacine (Intuniv®) and atomoxetine (Strattera®) (Lexicomp®, 2017). These medications do not tend to be as effective at controlling ADHD as the stimulant class, and they have their own range of side effects (CDC, 2017b; American Academy of Pediatrics, 2011).

An alternative to medications is behavioral therapy. The goals of behavioral therapy are to learn and reward positive behavior, both in and out of the classroom, and to decrease unwanted, negative behaviors. While some parents may choose behavioral therapy alone, it is important to note it is most successful when used in conjunction with a medication to treat ADHD (CDC, 2017b; American Academy of Pediatrics, 2011).

Anxiety and Depression

Another troubling concern regarding mental health of children in poverty is their risk of developing an anxiety or depressive disorder after early childhood. While the scope of this chapter is to describe pediatric medical conditions associated with poverty in early childhood, it is vital that educators realize that these children are at significant risk of later problems including psychiatric comorbidities (i.e., having two or more chronic conditions simultaneously) such as substance abuse if early interventions are not performed (Vine et al., 2012).

Economic disadvantage may play a significant role in developing anxiety. Children may be anxious about their food or housing instability, and poverty could be the stem of their anxiety, not mental illness. It is important to distinguish what is causing a child's anxiety, as it helps to predict the future anxiety burden. In addition, fear and anxiety are strong risk factors for developing depression. There is a wide range of treatment options including medications and behavioral therapy. For anxiety and depression, behavioral therapy is the first recommendation for treatment. Many mental health disorders also have a strong genetic component. Children in poverty may have additional barriers to treatment if their parents have such disorders, such as difficulty obtaining healthcare access, lower rates of diagnosis and treatment, and lower medication adherence. Educators should be aware of some of the main signs of these mental health disorders, including lack of participation and focus, a smaller social circle, and fewer interactions with peers. These students should be referred to a school counselor for targeted interventions and aid (Baer, Kim, & Wilkenfeld, 2012; Tracy et al. 2009).

Other Health Considerations

Oral Health

Children living in poverty have a significant risk of oral health disparities, especially in regard to untreated tooth decay. At greatest risk are children under the age of eight years, and children who are non-Hispanic, Black, and Mexican-American. Studies have shown that low-income children have higher rates of unmet dental needs and decreased rates of dental utilization. Worldwide, the WHO reports that 60–90% of school-aged children have dental cavities (WHO, 2012; CDC, 2017e).

The American Academy of Pediatric Dentistry released a report in 2014 discussing the tooth decay epidemic facing children in the United States. Most tooth decay is preventable. Without proper treatment, however, tooth decay can lead to long-term complications such as tooth damage and an increased lifetime risk of cavities and gum disease. In children, effects can be seen in regard to intellectual and social development such as speech problems, poor school performance, missed school, as well as severe pain for the child. This could be the result of pain that then becomes distracting in the school setting or lack of teeth due to decay causing alignment issues, resulting in speech problems and other difficulties (American Academy of Pediatric Dentistry, 2017).

Children living in poverty may not have access to dental care until they attend school. There are often school-based dental care and dental sealant programs available for children who do not receive routine dental care. These children could benefit greatly from sealants, which are thin, plastic coatings applied on the top, chewing surfaces of the teeth to help prevent cavities and tooth decay. Those who work with young children may hear complaints of tooth pain or notice children's trouble eating certain foods, which are warning signs of tooth decay or more significant tooth damage (CDC, 2017d; da Fonseca, 2012).

Lice

Louse infestations are a particular problem for children living in poor conditions and practicing poor personal hygiene. While there are three types of lice, the most common type in U.S. children is head or scalp lice.

Head lice can be identified by their color and presentation. Grown lice are usually brownish in color, but their nits are grayish white and attach to the hair. Head lice are more common in children with long hair, and they are spread through close contact. Examples of transmission include shared hairbrushes, combs, or headgear. The primary symptom is itching of the scalp, which can result in secondary infections. The American Academy of Pediatrics (AAP) states that most episodes of head lice are not acquired in school. While many schools have initiated "no-nit" policies regarding head lice, the AAP recommends against "no-nit" policies or sending children with head lice home (American Academy of Pediatrics, 2015). When a child is identified as having head lice, it is recommended that the whole family be treated. Treatment is available over-the-counter and includes permethrin- and pyrethrin-based products (Elimite™, Nix®, RID®) (Lexicomp®, 2017). However, there have been increasing cases of lice resistant to over-the-counter products, which then necessitate prescription medications such as ivermectin (Stromectol®) or spinosad (Natroba™) (Lexicomp®, 2017) for treatment. Beginning educators are usually told by school nurses or experienced teachers that children should not be sharing personal items such as hairbrushes, combs, or hats. For children living in low-income conditions, it is likely that they will not be able to afford treatment and are more likely to have more severe lice infestations (Devore & Schutze, 2015; American Academy of Pediatrics, 2015).

Lead Poisoning

Childhood lead poisoning affects approximately half a million American children aged one to five years. The CDC (2017h) reports that worldwide, more than four million households with children have high levels of lead exposure. Treatment is recommended for children with a documented blood lead level, as lead exposure can affect most systems in the body. Children may go untreated because they do not experience any obvious symptoms. Lead poisoning can be acute or chronic. Major sources of childhood lead exposure include lead found in soils, paints, food cans, gasoline, and drinking water from lead piping. Lead exposure is more common in low-income children due to environmental factors such as older housing and deteriorating playgrounds. Acute, high-dose lead poisoning can cause neurological problems including brain damage and coma. Long-term, chronic lead exposure can cause developmental delay, learning disabilities, abdominal pain, sleep problems, and irritability (CDC, 2017h; WHO, 2017a; Viver et al., 2011).

Immunizations

Many children living in poverty may be eligible for Medicaid, a type of governmental insurance, which provides health coverage to low-income children and adults. Medicaid and most other insurances cover routine vaccinations against vaccine-preventable diseases. Most health departments also provide this service at no to low cost to people without insurance, such as undocumented immigrants. Per the CDC, most children who follow the regular vaccination schedule will be immunized against most vaccine-preventable diseases by the age of two (CDC, 2017g). Low-income children who do not receive routine, preventive healthcare may not have completed all of their vaccinations in a timely manner. This can lead to an increased risk of disease and infections, as well as higher rates of emergency department visits and inpatient hospitalizations. One common example of concern is associated with the influenza vaccine that is recommended yearly for children over six months unless specific health circumstances prohibit vaccination. While low-income children may receive many of the recommended routine vaccinations, they may not receive the influenza vaccine yearly, making these children more prone to developing influenza and complications from the disease (*ChildTrends DataBank*, 2015; Klevens & Luman, 2001).

Access to Healthcare

It is important to note when considering the incidence and treatment of diseases affecting children living in poverty that their families may be unable to afford or access medications needed to treat or manage their conditions. This results in a disproportionate number of the children having undesirable healthcare outcomes. For example, researchers have reported higher degrees of morbidity in low-income children with certain medical conditions including asthma, cystic fibrosis, spina bifida, congenital heart disorders, diabetes type 1, autism, epilepsy, leukemias, HIV/AIDS, and end-of-life care (Pulcini, Zima, Kelleher, & Houtrow, 2017; Simkiss, Blackburn, Mukoro, Read, & Spencer, 2011; The National Academies Press, 2015; Beaune et al., 2014; Huynh, Henry, & Dosani, 2015; Hansen & Paintsil, 2016; Heagarty, 1991).

Children living in poverty are less likely to receive preventive care, and the diagnosis of chronic conditions may be delayed when compared to children from wealthier families. They have more emergency department visits and inpatient hospitalizations. In addition, they have limited access to medications. If they have prescription health and medication coverage through Medicaid or another insurance plan, they still may be unable to afford out-of-pocket expenses associated with healthcare. In general, this puts children at increased risk of medical complications. Well-known conditions associated with childhood poverty and disability include food insecurity, housing instability, and increased environmental hazards. Other factors such as inadequate mental health support and lack of prenatal care can significantly impact future childhood disability. The National Center for Children in Poverty names health disparities such as asthma, oral health, obesity, and maternal/fetal health as target areas of needed improvement (Stevens, Seid, Mistry, & Halfon, 2006).

A 2015 National Health Interview survey from the CDC stated that only 4.5% of children under the age of 18 years had no health insurance. Of the over 95% of children insured, 54.7% had private insurance and 42.2% had public insurance. Some children may have both private and public insurance for specific reasons such as adoption assistance, disability assistance for chronic conditions, diseases, or cancers. Even with this high number of insured children, there is still a significant problem concerning access to healthcare services. Barriers to access include working parents, limited number of primary care physicians, limited weekend and evening hours, and scarcity of school medical clinics (American Academy of Pediatrics, 2017b; Racine, 2016).

Healthcare professionals and educators should consider a child's immigration status in relation to their access to healthcare. Immigrant families are more likely to be low-income even though they have high employment rates. Immigrants are more likely to receive low wages compared to their native-born counterparts, and they also have lower levels of health insurance (Borjas, 2011; Dreyer, 2017; van Hook, 2003).

The cycle of poverty is a vicious one that is difficult to break, and many low-income children may have parents who were in this cycle as children. In addition, some parents may have decreased health literacy, which can hinder healthcare access (American Academy of Pediatrics, 2017a; Benjamin, 2010).

Conclusion

Those who work with children must continue to consider what pediatric medical conditions are associated with poverty and how these disorders may impact upon their pupils. Intervention strategies including increased funding for more extensive health insurance coverage and enhanced access to health services for poor children, along with the provision of comprehensive medical care, have had positive impacts. A great deal more, however, needs to be done as current outcomes must improve. The use of a team approach for the care of poor children with health issues continues to receive interest (Racine, 2016). Teachers are key members of this team, and by working closely with healthcare providers, parents, and guardians, they can have a positive impact in overcoming health challenges encountered in low-income communities.

References

American Academy of Pediatric Dentistry (2017). The state of little teeth. Retrieved from www.aapd.org/assets/1/7/State_of_Little_Teeth_Final.pdf.

American Academy of Pediatrics (2011). Subcommittee on Attention-Deficit/ Hyperactivity Disorder. ADHD: Clinical practice guideline for the diagnosis, evaluation, and treatment of attention-deficit/hyperactivity disorder in children and adolescents. *Pediatrics*, *128*(5), 1–16. doi: 10.1542/peds.2011-2654.

American Academy of Pediatrics (2015). AAP updates: Treatments for head lice. Retrieved from www.aap.org/en-us/about-the-aap/aap-press-room/pages/aap-updates-treatments- for-head-lice.aspx.

American Academy of Pediatrics (2016). Council on community pediatrics, policy statement: Poverty and child health in the United States. *Pediatrics*, *137*(4), 1–14. doi: 10.1542/peds.2016-0339.

American Academy of Pediatrics (2017a). Health literacy and pediatrics. Retrieved from www.aap.org/en-us/professional-resources/Research/research-resources/Pages/Health-Literacy-and-Pediatrics.aspx.

American Academy of Pediatrics (2017b). Poverty & child health. Retrieved from www.aap.org/en-us/advocacy-and-policy/aap-health- initiatives/poverty/Pages/home.aspx.

American College of Allergy, Asthma, and Immunology (2014). Children and allergies. Retrieved from http://acaai.org/allergies/who-has-allergies/children-allergies.

Baer, J. C., Kim, M. S., & Wilkenfeld, B. (2012). Is it generalized anxiety disorder or poverty? An examination of poor mothers and their children. *Child and Adolescent Social Work Journal*, *29*(4), 345–355. doi: 10.1007/s10560-012-0263-3.

Barnes, K. C., Grant, A. V., Hansel, N. N., Gao, P., & Dunston, G. M. (2007). Americans with asthma: Genetic insights. *Proceedings to the American Thoracic Society*, *4*, 58–68. doi: 10.1513/pats.200607-146JG.

Beaune, L., Leavens, A., Muskat, B., Ford-Jones, L., Rapoport, A., Zlotnik-Shaul, R., Morinis, J., & Chapman, L. A. (2014). Poverty and pediatric palliative care: What can we do? *Journal of Social Work in End-of-Life & Palliative Care*, *10*(2), 170–185. doi: 10.1080/15524256.2014.906375.

Benjamin, R. M. (2010). Improving health by improving health literacy. *Public Health Reports*, *125*(6), 784–785. doi: 10.1177/003335491012500602.

Borjas, G. J. (2011). Poverty and program participation among immigrant children. *The Future of Children*, *21*(1), 247–266.

Brooks-Gunn, J., & Duncan, G. J. (1997). The effects of poverty on children. *The Future of Children*, 7(2), 55–77.

Brozek, J. L., Bousquet, J., Baena-Cagnani, C. E., Bonini, S., Canonica, G. W., Casale, T. B., van Wijk, R. G., Ohta, K., Zuberbier, T., & Schünemann, H. J.. (2017). Allergic rhinitis and its impact on asthma (ARIA) guidelines: 2016 revision. *Journal of Allergy and Clinical Immunology*, *140*(4), 950–958. doi: 10.1016/j.jaci.2017.03.050.

CBS News (2017). Mylan CEO on EpiPen drug price controversy. Retrieved from www.cbsnews.com/news/epipen-price-hike-controversy-mylan-ceo-heather-bresch-speaks-out.

Centers for Disease Control and Prevention (2017a). ADHD: Data & statistics. Retrieved from www.cdc.gov/ncbddd/adhd/data.html.

Centers for Disease Control and Prevention (2017b). ADHD: Treatment. Retrieved from www.cdc.gov/ncbddd/adhd/treatment.html.

Centers for Disease Control and Prevention (2017c). Childhood obesity facts. Retrieved from www.cdc.gov/obesity/data/childhood.html.

Centers for Disease Control and Prevention (2017d). Children's oral health. Retrieved from www.cdc.gov/oralhealth/children_adults/child.htm.

Centers for Disease Control and Prevention (2017e). Disparities in oral health. Retrieved from www.cdc.gov/oralhealth/oral_health_disparities/index.htm.

Centers for Disease Control and Prevention (2017f). Health insurance coverage. Retrieved from www.cdc.gov/nchs/fastats/health-insurance.htm.

Centers for Disease Control and Prevention (2017g). Immunizations schedules. Retrieved from www.cdc.gov/vaccines/schedules/hcp/child-adolescent.html.

Centers for Disease Control and Prevention (2017h). Lead. Retrieved from www. cdc.gov/nceh/lead.

Centers for Disease Control and Prevention (2017i). Most recent asthma data. Retrieved from www.cdc.gov/asthma/most_recent_data.htm.

Centers for Disease Control and Prevention (2017j). Obesity and socioeconomic status in children and adolescents. Retrieved from www.cdc.gov/nchs/products/databriefs/db51.htm.

ChildTrends DataBank (2014). ADHD: Indicators of child and youth well-being. Retrieved from www.childtrends.org/wp-content/uploads/2014/08/76_ADHD.pdf.

ChildTrends DataBank (2015). Immunizations. Retrieved from www.childtrends.org/wp-content/uploads/2015/12/17_Immunization.pdf.

Ciaccio C. E., DiDonna, A., Kennedy, K., Barnes, C. S., Portnoy, J. M., & Rosenwasser, L. J. (2014). Secondhand tobacco smoke exposure in low-income children and its association with asthma. *Allergy & Asthma Proceedings*, *35*(6), 462–466. doi: 10.2500/aap.2014.35.3788.

Courtney, A. U., McCarter, D. F., & Pollart, S. M. (2005). Childhood asthma: Treatment update. *American Family Physician*, *71*(10), 1959–1968. Retrieved from www.aafp.org/afp/2005/0515/p1959.html.

Crystal-Peters, J., Neslusan, C., Crown, W. H., & Torres, A. (2002). Treating allergic rhinitis in patients with comorbid asthma: The risk of asthma-related hospitalizations and emergency department visits. *Journal of Allergy and Clinical Immunology*, *109*(1), 57–62. doi: 10.1067/mai.2002.120554.

da Fonseca, M. A. (2012). The effects of poverty on children's development and oral health. *Pediatric Dentistry*, *34*(1), 32–38.

Devore, C. D., Schutze, G. E., & The Council on School Health and Committee on Infectious Diseases (2015). Clinical report: Head lice. *Pediatrics*, *135*(5), e1355–1356, Errata *136*(4), 781–782. doi: 10.1542/peds.2015-0746.

Dileepan, K., & Feldt, M. M. (2013). Type 2 diabetes mellitus in children and adolescents. *Pediatrics in Review*, *34*(12), 541–548. doi: 10.1542/pir.34-12-541.

Dreyer, B. (2017). Immigration children: General issues. Retrieved from NYU School of Medicine, https://med.nyu.edu/pediatrics/developmental/benard-dreyer-md/my-positions-key-issues-aap-members/childhood-poverty.

Eichengield, L. F., Boguniewicz, M., Simpson, E. L., Russell, J. J., Block, J. K., Feldman, S. R., Clark, A. R., Tofte, S., Dunn, J. D., & Paller, A. S. (2015). Translating atopic dermatitis management guidelines into practice for primary care providers. *Pediatrics*, *136*(3), 1–12. doi: 10.1542/peds.2014-3678.

Gregory, J. M., Moore, D. J., & Simmons, J. H. (2013). Type 1 diabetes mellitus. *Pediatrics in Review*, *34*(5), 203–215. doi: 10.1542/pir.34-5-203.

Hansen, C., & Paintsil, E. (2016). Infectious diseases of poverty in children: A tale of two worlds. *Pediatrics Clinics of North America*, *63*(1), 37–66. doi: 10.1016/j.pcl.2015.08.002.

Heagarty, M. C. (1991). Pediatric acquired immunodeficiency syndrome, poverty, and national priorities. *American Journal of Diseases of Children, 145*(5), 527–528. doi: 10.1001/archpedi.1991.02160050053012.

Huynh, L., Henry, B., & Dosani, N. (2015). Minding the gap: Access to palliative care and the homeless. *BMC Palliative Care, 14*(62), 1–4. doi: 10.1186/s12904-015-0059-2.

Johnson, D. D., & Johnson, B. (2006). *High stakes: Poverty, testing, and failure in American schools* (2nd ed.). New York: Rowman & Littlefield.

Klevens, R. M., & Luman, E. T. (2001). U.S. children living in and near poverty: Risk of vaccine-preventable diseases. *American Journal of Preventative Medicine, 20*(4, supplemental), 41–46. doi: http://dx.doi.org/10.1016/S0749-3797(01)00281-1.

Knoell, K. A., & Greer, K. E. (1999). Atopic dermatitis. *Pediatrics in Review, 20*(2), 46–52. doi: 10.1542/pir.20-2-46.

Levine, J. A. (2011). Poverty and obesity in the U.S. *Diabetes, 60*(11), 2667–2668. doi: 10.2337/db11-1118.

Lexicomp Online®, Pediatric and Neonatal Lexi-Drugs® (2017, July 2). *Wolters Kluwer Clinical Drug Information*. Hudson, OH: Lexi-Comp®, Inc.

Link, H. W. (2014). Pediatric asthma in a nutshell. *Pediatrics in Review, 35*(7), 287–298. doi: 10.1542/pir.35-7-287.

Lyons, J. J., Milner, J. D., & Stone, K. D. (2015). Atopic dermatitis in children: Clinical features, pathophysiology, and treatment. *Immunology and Allergy Clinics of North America, 35*(1), 161–183. doi: 10.1016/j.iac.2014.09.008.

Mahr, T. A., & Sheth, K. (2005). Update on allergic rhinitis. *Pediatrics in Review, 26*(8), 284–289. doi: 10.1542/pir.26-8-284.

Nicholas, K. A. (2016). Children, poverty and the burden of disease: Impacts on community health centers. *Washington Association of Community Migrant Health Centers, 16*(3, supplemental), s83–89.

Pacheco, C. M., Ciaccio, C. E., Nazir, N., Daley, C. M., DiDonna, A., Choi, W. S., Barnes, C. S., & Rossenwasser, L. J. (2014). Homes of low-income minority families with asthmatic children have increased condition issues. *Allergy & Asthma Proceedings, 35*(6), 467–474. doi: 10.2500/aap.2014.35.3792.

Potter, P. C. (2010). Current guidelines for the management of asthma in young children. *Asthma, Allergy, and Immunology Research Journal, 2*(1), 1–13. doi: 10.4168/aair.2010.2.1.1.

Pulcini, C. D., Zima, B. T., Kelleher, K., & Houtrow, A. J. (2017). Poverty and trends in three common chronic disorders. *Pediatrics, 139*(3), 1–10. doi: 10.1542/peds.2016-2539.

Racine, A. D. (2016). Child poverty and the health care system. *Academic Pediatrics, 16*(3, supplemental), s83–89. doi: 10.1016/j.acap.2015.12.002.

Rogers, R., Eagle, T. F., Sheetz, A., Woodward, A., Leibowitz, R., Song, M. K., Sylvester, R., Corriveau, N., Kline-Rogers, E., Jiang, Q., Jackson, E. A., & Eagle, K. A. (2015). The relationship between childhood obesity, low socioeconomic status, and race/ethnicity. *Journal of Childhood Obesity, 11*(6), 691–695. doi: 10.1089/chi.2015.0029.

Russell, A. E., Ford, T., & Russell, G. (2015). Socioeconomic associations with ADHD: Findings from a mediation analysis. *Public Library of Science*. doi: 10.1371/journal.pone.0128248.

Silber, J. H., Rosenbaum, P. R., Calhoun, S. R., Reiter, J. G., Hill, A. S., Guevara, J. P., Zorc, J. J., & Even-Shoshan, O. (2017). Racial disparities in Medicaid asthma hospitalizations. *Pediatrics, 139*(1), 1–12. doi: 10.1542/peds.2016-1221.

Simkiss, D. E., Blackburn, C. M., Mukoro, F. O., Read, J. M., & Spencer, N. J. (2011). Childhood disability and socio-economic circumstances in low and middle-income countries: Systematic review. *BMC Pediatrics, 11*(119), 1–15. doi: 10. 1186/1471-2431-11-119.

Stevens, G. D., Seid, M., Mistry, R., & Halfon, N. (2006). Disparities in primary care for vulnerable children: The influence of multiple risk factors. *Health Services Research Journal, 41*(2), 507–511. doi: 0.1111/j.1475-6773.2005.00498.x.

The National Academy Press (2015). Poverty and childhood disability. In *Mental disorders and disabilities among low-income children* (pp. 105–123). Washington, DC: The National Academy Press. doi: 10.17226/21780.

Tollefson, M., & Bruckner, A. L. (2014). Atopic dermatitis: Skin-directed management. *Pediatrics in Review, 134*(6): e1735–e1744. doi: 10.1542/peds.2014-2812.

Tracy, M., Zimmerman, F. J., Galea, S., McCauley, E., & Stoep, A. V. (2009). What explains the relation between family poverty and childhood depressive symptoms? *Journal of Psychiatric Research, 42*(14), 1163–1175. doi: 10.1016/j. jpsychires.2008.01.011.

UNICEF (2017). Undernutrition contributes to nearly half of all deaths in children under 5 and is widespread in Asia and Africa. Retrieved from https://data. unicef.org/topic/nutrition/malnutrition.

van Hook, J. (2003). Poverty grows among children of immigrants in U.S. Retrieved from www.migrationpolicy.org/article/poverty-grows-among-children-immigrants-us.

Vine, M., Stoep, A. V., Bell, J., Rhew, I. C., Gudmundsen, G., & McCauley, E. (2012). Associations between household and neighborhood income and anxiety symptoms in young adolescents including psychiatric comorbidities such as substance abuse. *Depression and Anxiety, 29*(9), 824–832. doi: 10.1002/da.21948.

Viver, P. M., Hauptman, M., Weitzen, S. H., Bell, S., Quilliam, D. N., & Logan, J. R. (2011). The important health impact of where a child lives: Neighborhood characteristics and the burden of lead poisoning. *Maternal and Child Health Journal, 15*(8), 1195–1202. doi: 10.1007/s10995-010-0692-6.

World Health Organization (2012). Oral health. Retrieved from www.who.int/ mediacentre/factsheets/fs318/en.

World Health Organization (2017a). Childhood lead poisoning. Retrieved from www.who.int/ceh/publications/leadguidance.pdf.

World Health Organization (2017b). Global database on child growth and malnutrition. Retrieved from www.who.int/nutgrowthdb/about/introduction/en.

World Health Organization (2017c). Micronutrient deficiencies. Retrieved from www.who.int/nutrition/topics/vad/en.

5 Business and Economics

The Transformative Potential of Marketing to Fight Child Poverty

Fabienne T. Cadet, Dan Rubin, and Joan Ball

Introduction

The past three decades in marketing research and practice have witnessed a shift in focus from mere value exchange between firms and customers to a growing interest in customer experience and well-being. While customer satisfaction and its relationship to customer loyalty, repeat purchase behavior, and positive word-of-mouth have long been of interest to marketers (see Armstrong & Kotler, 2017, for review), interest in consumer well-being in other domains (e.g., health, safety, work, family, leisure, and finance) is nascent to the field (Sirgy, Lee, & Rahtz, 2007). Distinct bodies of literature under the banners of transformative consumer research (Mick, Pettigrew, Pechmann, & Ozanne, 2012) and transformative service research (Mick, 2006) have begun to address the relationship between marketing and consumer well-being in ways that have the potential to influence marketing theory, practice, and consumer outcomes. Moreover, as marketing and consumer behavior researchers continue to explore marketplace value creation beyond exchange relationships, the potential for marketing to contribute positively to consumer well-being increases. The purpose of this chapter is to examine these emerging streams of research in the context of one well-being outcome—specifically, the transformative potential of marketing to fight child poverty.

Child Poverty: A Worldwide Challenge

Bottom/Base of the Pyramid (BoP) has become the standard description for the approximately two thirds of the world's population who live on the equivalent of less than nine $US per day (Arnold & Valentin, 2013). For these people, limited access to/inadequate basic service systems leaves them with limited or no access to health care, education, transportation, electricity, sanitation, quality food, drinking water, and adequate housing (Fisk et al., 2016). Child poverty is not, however, exclusive to BoP countries. One in five children in high-income countries live in relative income poverty as measured by factors such as education, mental health, alcohol abuse, economic opportunities, and the environment (UNICEF Office of Research, 2017).

Indeed, nearly 40% of American children spend at least one year in poverty before they turn 18 (Children International, 2017). Moreover, approximately 15 million children in the United States live at or below the poverty level (National Center for Children in Poverty, 2017). Thus, childhood poverty is a worldwide crisis that has been shown to be a substantial threat to children's well-being (National Center for Children in Poverty, 2017).

Outcomes of child poverty include delinquency, academic achievement deficits, and mental health consequences (Nikulina, Widom, & Czaja, 2011). Growing up in a poor household and/or poor neighborhood may predispose a child to experience more traumas and to have fewer resources to buffer the negative impact of traumatic experiences, which in turn may contribute to a range of difficulties (Nikulina, Widom, & Czaja, 2011). Poverty is associated with a variety of conditions (e.g., substandard housing and homelessness, poor nutrition and healthcare, unsafe neighborhoods, and under-resourced schools) that negatively impact children, families, and communities (American Psychological Association, 2017). Thus, whether found in BoP countries or the developed world, poverty has been shown to be a substantial threat to children's well-being and societal flourishing (National Center for Children in Poverty, 2017).

But how might the field of marketing help improve well-being among children in poverty and their families? Before describing how marketing can contribute to efforts to address childhood poverty, it is important to clarify what is meant by the term "marketing."

What Is Marketing?

A simple definition of marketing is engaging customers and managing profitable customer relationships (Armstrong & Kotler, 2017). According to Armstrong and Kotler (2017), the marketing process consists of five steps:

1   Understanding the marketplace and customers,
2   Designing marketing strategies with customers in mind,
3   Creating and delivering value,
4   Building profitable relationships with customers, and
5   Capturing value from customers.

These steps are executed across what Armstrong and Kotler refer to as the "marketing mix" (i.e., Product, Price, Place, and Promotion (see Armstrong & Kotler, 2017, for review). These "4Ps" represent the traditional exchange view of marketing embraced for most of the 20th century (Grönroos, 1994).

The Shift to Transformative Marketing

New marketing theories and disciplines emerged from traditional exchange models in the latter part of the 20th and early 21st centuries that shifted marketing focus from firm-centric approaches to value exchange to an increased interest in the needs and behaviors of consumers. At the beginning of the 1970s, for instance, the marketing of services emerged with concepts and models geared to the unique characteristics of service versus product marketing (Grönroos, 1994). Social marketing, which appeared in the literature at the same time, focused on the effect of marketing on social behaviors to benefit the firm, the target audience, and the general society (Weinreich, 2017). This work laid the groundwork for the emergence of relationship marketing in the 1980s and 1990s, which marked a paradigm shift in marketing from a focus on transactions to the view that the firm and its customers benefit when in relationship (Palmatier, 2008). Transformative consumer research and transformative service research extended this notion to how poor individuals participate in marketplace exchange, which has the potential to inform broader discourses related to how best to provide needed resources and access to goods and services in contemporary society. This underscores our thesis that, as an institution, marketing can play a pivotal role in ensuring customer welfare and achieving related social and environmental ends (Heath & Chatzidakis, 2012).

Transformative Consumer Research: An Overview

The primary aim of transformative consumer research (TCR) is "to improve well-being, which is a state of flourishing that involves health, happiness, and prosperity" (Mick, Pettigrew, Pechmann, & Ozanne, 2012, p. 6). Concerning poverty alleviation, TCR scholarship aims for deeper scientific understanding of poverty that can be translated into practice that helps improve the material, social, and cultural conditions of the poor (Blocker et al., 2013). Broad conceptualizations of poverty open the door for consumer research to have a voice in the multidisciplinary poverty dialogue. In particular, TCR builds upon the notion that consumption can be linked to well-being (Blocker et al., 2013).

With its aim to improve consumer well-being, TCR has the potential to complement an evolving conceptualization of poverty by shedding light on aspects of consumption and consumer well-being and, in the process, to accelerate the achievement of transformative outcomes for the poor (Blocker et al., 2013). In addition to identifying practical opportunities to pursue well-being, the TCR lens offers a platform for inspiring consumer researchers to reach for transformative impact through prescribing an explicit, consumer well-being agenda (Blocker et al., 2013). Moreover, TCR can provide policy makers and the development community with insights toward achieving long-standing aims of improving the lives of people living in poverty.

Specifically, by seeing the poor as individuals who are making myriad consumption decisions that can be analyzed using robust consumer theories, methods, and perspectives, this stream of research helps to deepen our understanding of poverty (Blocker et al., 2013). TCR can illuminate, for example, "how income-poor individuals participate in marketplace exchange, which in turn could add insights to the broader discourses related to resource assets versus deficits, or access versus restrictions to goods and services in contemporary society" (Blocker et al., 2011, p. 3). This, according to Blocker and colleagues (2011), would help advance the dialogue beyond debates of "poor incomes" versus "poor living" to incorporate the everyday lived experiences of millions of poor consumers, the strategies they employ, and the resources they tap into as they manage day-to-day.

The birth of the TCR movement challenges the macroeconomic approach to consumer welfare, redefining customer well-being as the alignment of "individual and societal needs" (i.e., physical, psychological, economic, social) as they relate to consumption (Pancer & Handelman, 2012). TCR illuminates how income-poor individuals participate in marketplace exchange, which in turn could add insights to the broader discourses related to resource assets versus deficits, or access versus restrictions to goods and services in contemporary society (Blocker et al., 2011).

More recently, a related but distinct stream of research has emerged within the field of marketing. After first being introduced at the TCR conference in 2011, transformative service research (TSR) has grown into an independent research stream. While consumer behavior research gave rise to TCR, TSR is an extension of service research. Services dominate the lives of consumers today. However, to a large extent, TCR does not address the role of services in affecting consumer well-being (Anderson et al., 2013). Furthermore, traditional service research rarely considers outcomes related to consumer well-being (Anderson et al., 2013).

Transformative Service Research

Transformative service research (TSR) focuses on improving consumer and societal welfare through service. It is inspired by transformative consumer research that seeks to solve "real" problems of consumers by applying marketing techniques and tools to enhance the lives of individuals and communities (see Rosenbaum et al., 2011). First conceptualized by Anderson (2010), today we regard TSR as any research, regardless of academic discipline, that, at its core, investigates the relationship between service and well-being (Anderson & Ostrom, 2015). TSR links service and TCR and focuses on well-being outcomes related to services (Gebauer & Reynoso, 2013). As a research paradigm, TSR is defined as "service research that centers on creating uplifting changes and improvements in the well-being of individuals (consumers and employees), families, social networks, communities, cities, nations, collectives, and ecosystems" (Rosenbaum et al., 2011, p. 3).

TSR draws from service-focused well-being research and emanates from numerous disciplines and sub-disciplines including TCR (Mick, 2006) and social marketing that focuses on creating well-being-oriented behavioral change (Andreasen, 2002). TSR not only seeks to understand the problems but also strives to identify community strengths to develop service strategies, innovations, and designs that build better futures (Fisk et al., 2016).

TSR prioritizes well-being among poorer consumers and ethnic minorities, well-being at the collective levels, the impact of co-creation on employee well-being, and sustainable relationships among social, economic, and environmental systems (Anderson et al., 2013). In the case of poverty, issues abound such as access to services, marginalization during service experiences, lack of service literacy, and discrimination embedded in service designs (Fisk et al., 2016). In this chapter, we focus on market-based approaches to solving the long-term causes of such poverty.

Market-Based Solutions Addressing Child Poverty

Hammond and Prahalad (2004) contend that there are several payoffs for the poor when private enterprises participate in the BoP market (Jaiswal & Gupta, 2015). These payoffs include the opportunity to consume newer products and services, avail wider consumption options, and a greater capacity to consume that, in turn, enhance their overall quality of life (Jaiswal & Gupta, 2015). The private sector can play a "key role in poverty alleviation by viewing the poor as producers, and emphasize buying from them, rather than selling to them" (Karnani, 2007, p. 102). Adoption of this view would necessitate a paradigm shift in the way that critical services are provided to the poor as they are currently a stumbling block, potentially preventing the poor from realizing increases in real income. Drawing from the TSR literature, we view the 4 As model of marketing as providing a useful framework for marketing to and with low-income individuals.

The 4 As of Marketing

In contrast to the traditional exchange model represented by the 4Ps of marketing described earlier, Sheth and Sisodia (2012) propose a consumer-centric framework—the 4As—that is relevant to better serving low-income individuals in the marketplace. The 4As (Acceptability, Affordability, Accessibility, Awareness) are geared toward identifying the needs and marketplace opportunities related to low-income individuals, especially in rural areas. Prahalad (2004) applied the 4As framework to BoP consumers to show that, despite research to the contrary, sound marketing principles are not always applied to practices geared toward lower-income consumers. Prahalad's 4As framework is a tool that helps marketers align their actions with the four essential values sought by customers. We believe this framework holds great potential for strategic approaches to alleviating childhood poverty. These values can be summarized as:

- Acceptability: the extent to which the firm's total product offering meets and exceeds customer expectations. It has two dimensions: functional acceptability and psychological acceptability.
- Affordability: the extent to which customers can pay the product's price. It has two dimensions: economic affordability (ability to pay) and psychological affordability (willingness to pay).
- Accessibility: the extent to which customers can readily acquire and use the product. It has two dimensions: availability and convenience.
- Awareness: the extent to which customers are informed regarding product characteristics, persuaded to try it, and, if applicable, reminded to repurchase it. It has two dimensions: brand awareness and product knowledge (Sheth & Sisodia, 2012).

In applying the 4As framework to existing practices and institutions, it is apparent that services for many impoverished people frequently do not meet these standards. The inadequate provision of these critical services perpetuates poverty generationally and thus addressing them should be a priority in the fight against childhood poverty.

Sound Marketing Practice: Improve Marketplace Services for the Poor

Since 2000, areas of concentrated poverty—those in which at least 40% of the population are living below the poverty threshold—have increased significantly (Iceland & Hernandez, 2017). In these areas, people are often cut off from essential resources required for income generation and maintaining a sufficient quality of life. According to Iceland and Hernandez (2017), services such as law enforcement, supermarkets, financial institutions, transportation, health care, and education tend to be either of inferior quality or wholly absent in these environments. Consequently, the lack of these services has been shown to contribute significantly to the ill effects of poverty on children. For example, without access to nutrient-rich foods and recreational opportunities provided by outdoor play (due to poor maintenance of parks and sidewalks or safety concerns from high crime rates), children raised in areas of concentrated poverty show significantly higher rates of obesity. In fact, every 1% decrease in familial income status increases the chances of a child becoming obese by 1.17% (Rogers et al., 2015). Research supports that such structural barriers in areas of concentrated poverty act as an impediment to upward social mobility (Iceland & Hernandez, 2017).

Access to services such as child care can be transformative and can offer an intergenerational mechanism by which to eliminate child poverty. The provision of such services by institutions of marketing can have positive benefits for employees, society at large, and the institutions themselves. Employer-sponsored child care improves employee engagement, retention, recruitment, loyalty, and productivity (Bright Horizons, 2016).

Additionally, studies demonstrate that the provision of high-quality child care benefits children's cognitive and social development (National Women's Law Center, 2016). According to the National Center for Children in Poverty (2017):

> The family's largest single expense—greater even than the cost of housing—is the cost of child care. Reliable care is critical for working parents, and high-quality care is essential for children's development. For low-income children, it can help bridge the achievement gap between them and their more affluent peers. But the high cost puts reliable, quality care out of reach for many of the families who need it most.
>
> (paragraph 1)

With such exorbitant costs, low-income families are often forced to rely on more informal child care arrangements (Child Care Aware of America, 2014). Coupled with the facts that social support systems have been shown to be less reliable in areas of concentrated poverty and that poor working parents are more likely to work unconventional or unpredictable hours in which child care is often not available, it is clear that child care is a roadblock for low-income families. Applying the 4As lens to the provision of these services, it becomes apparent that the principles of accessibility and affordability are being violated in relation to the delivery of services to the poor.

Potential Marketplace Solutions: The Case of Minority-Owned Business Services

To understand the potentially transformative impact of service delivery according to sound marketing practices, we can look to the impact of accessible and affordable financial services to minority entrepreneurs. Minority-owned businesses represent 29% of all firms in the United States, yet only 11% have paid employees (Minority Business Development Agency [MBDA], 2017). According to the U.S. Department of Commerce's Minority Business Development Agency (2017), the achievement of entrepreneurial parity between minority and non-minority-owned businesses would result in the creation of an additional 13 million jobs. Further, The Center for Global Policy Solutions estimates that discrimination has led to 1.1 million fewer businesses owned by people of color, which would translate to 9 million jobs and $300 billion toward the national income (Austin, 2016).

These findings are especially significant as it is estimated that child poverty in the United States would be reduced by 72% if adults in low-income families with children had year-round, full-time employment (Hederman & Rector, 2003). Considering that access to capital is among the predominant sources of inequity for minority business owners, marketing can create solutions for such imbalances. According to the MBDA (2017):

- Minority firms are more likely to be denied loans at a rate nearly three times higher than non-minority firms
- Minority firms are likely to pay higher interest rates; on average 7.8%, while non-minority firms pay on average 6.4%
- Minority firms are less likely to receive loans; and when approved, receive lower loan amounts.

Stoll and colleagues (2004) argue that increases in black managers or business owners would serve to increase the employment rates of blacks across the board significantly. Reducing these barriers to entry through greater access to financial services should be a priority in the fight against child poverty. By looking at exemplars of companies that have provided financial services that are accessible and affordable, we can observe the transformative potential of the provision of services according to sound marketing principles. OneUnited Bank, the largest black-owned bank in the United States, invests heavily in low-income communities and supports driving economic growth in black communities through movements such as #BankBlack and #BuyBlack. Broadway Federal Bank, another black-owned financial institution, has the following mission statement:

> The Bank's mission is to serve the real estate, business and financial needs of customers in underserved urban communities with a commitment to excellent service, profitability and sustained growth. It also has a broader commitment to employ, train and mentor community residents, to contract for services with community businesses, and to encourage its management and staff to serve as volunteers in civic, community and religious organizations.
>
> (Broadway Federal Bank, 2017)

It is also worth considering that widespread acceptance of the traditional BoP proposition might interfere with entrepreneurship among the poor. Karnani's (2007) assertion that "MNCs [multinational corporations] might otherwise inhibit the emergence of local private entrepreneurs who provide economic as well as non-economic benefits to society (e.g., as community leaders)" (p. 96) is applicable domestically as well as abroad. His position acknowledges the positive societal benefits of the poor as producers—a proposition that is supported by numerous real-world examples.

Marketplace Solutions: The Case of Eastern Bank

For Eastern Bank Chairman and CEO Bob Rivers, the wealth gap revelation was a call to arms of sorts. Through the new initiative, Eastern Bank is stepping up with a $10 million growth fund aimed at providing loans to build the capacity of businesses owned by people of color. The 2015 Federal Reserve "Color of Wealth" report found that while white households have a median wealth of $247,500, blacks and Dominicans' median wealth is close to zero (Miller, 2017). Because small businesses are widely seen as the engines of the United States economy, Lloyd says, investing in them can help increase incomes in the communities where they're located (Miller, 2017). Currently, minority-owned businesses receive less than 2% of all venture capital in the United States. Ultimately, Rivers says, helping the business community serve people of color will contribute to improving the long-term economic well-being of the city (Miller, 2017).

Marketplace Solutions: The Case of Starbucks

On the heels of the launch of the private-sector-led 100,000 Opportunities Initiative to increase hiring of America's opportunity youth, Starbucks (NASDAQ: SBUX) announced two key strategic initiatives to support economic development and social change in diverse, urban communities by helping young people connect with meaningful employment and pathways to success (Rojas, 2017). "A new generation of young people—especially in low-income communities—are at risk for never, ever having a job," said Congressman Bobby L. Rush of the 1st District of Illinois (Starbucks, 2015, paragraph 9). "These young people are often neglected, especially those who are no longer in school or unable to find jobs and are not being trained to be productive citizens in the workplace" (Starbucks, 2015, paragraph 9).

This public/private service model is part of Starbuck's initiative to invest in at least 15 underserved communities across the U.S. by 2018 (Rojas, 2017) and an example of how such partnerships can provide resources to impoverished communities. Company officials say their goal is to contribute to the city's economic development and create job opportunities for local youth (Rojas, 2017). Starbucks plans to work with local minority-owned businesses to help with the construction and supply products for the store.

Conclusion

Despite ongoing efforts to combat child poverty, it remains a crisis in the United States and abroad. The academic community has demonstrated an interest in consumer well-being outcomes through research movements such as TCR and more recently TSR. We can look to these streams of research for practical solutions to addressing not just the symptoms of child poverty but also the long-term causes.

In applying the 4 As model of marketing to the provision of services to the poor, we see that essential services such as daycare and financial services are unaffordable and inaccessible to people living in poverty. As increasing real income is the only way to reduce poverty in general, we highlight these particular services, as they are likely to increase the number of jobs in areas of concentrated poverty and the ability of impoverished people to hold them. Given the potential of these services to eliminate poverty intergenerationally, we outline market-based solutions to provide them to the poor with sound marketing principles.

References

American Psychological Association. (2017). Effects of poverty, hunger and homelessness on children and youth. Retrieved from www.apa.org/pi/families/poverty.aspx.

Anderson, L., & Ostrom, A. L. (2015). Transformative service research: Advancing our knowledge about service and well-being. *Journal of Service Research*, *18*(3), 243–249.

Anderson, L., Ostrom, A., Corus, C., Fisk, R., Gallan, A., Giraldo, M., . . . Shirahada, K. (2013). Transformative service research: An agenda for the future. *Journal of Business Research*, *66*(8), 1203–1210.

Anderson, L. (2010). Improving well-being through transformative service: Moving forward and making a difference: Research priorities for the science of service. *Journal of Service Research*, *13*(1), 4–36.

Andreasen, A. R. (2002). Marketing social marketing in the social change marketplace. *Journal of Public Policy and Marketing*, *21*(1), 3–13.

Armstrong, G., & Kotler, P. (2017). *Marketing: An introduction.* New York: Pearson Education.

Arnold, D., & Valentin, A. (2013). Corporate social responsibility at the base of the pyramid. *Journal of Business Research*, *66*(10), 1904–1914.

Austin, A. (2016). *The color of entrepreneurship: Why the racial gap among firms costs the U.S. billions.* Retrieved from Center for Global Policy Solutions website: http://globalpolicysolutions.org/report/color-entrepreneurship-racial-gap-among-firms-costs-u-s-billions/#_edn33.

Blocker, C., Ruth, J. A., Sridharan, S., Beckwith, C., Ekici, A., Goudie-Hutton, M., . . . Varman, R. (2011). Applying a transformative consumer research lens to understanding and alleviating poverty. *Journal of Research for Consumers*, *19*, 1–9.

Blocker, C., Ruth, J. A., Sridharan, S., Beckwith, C., Ekici, A., Goudie-Hutton, M., . . . Varman, R. (2013). Understanding poverty and promoting poverty alleviation through transformative consumer research. *Journal of Business Research*, *66*, 1195–1202.

Bright Horizons. (2016). The lasting impact of employer-sponsored child care centers. Retrieved from https://solutionsatwork.brighthorizons.com/-/media/bh/saw/pdfs/childcare/2016_lasting-impact-child-care.ashx?la=en&hash=90C78FE8C1BC7C604743CF1AF57F6D961ABAAA01.

Broadway Federal Bank. (2017). *Mission Statement.* Retrieved from Broadway Federal Bank website: www.broadwayfederalbank.com/history.

Child Care Aware of America. (2014). *Parents and the high cost of child care: 2014 Report.* Retrieved from National Conference of State Legislatures website: www.ncsl.org/documents/cyf/2014_Parents_and_the_High_Cost_of_Child_Care.pdf.

Children International. (2017). *Child poverty in the U.S.* Retrieved from www.children.org/global-poverty/global-poverty-facts/facts-about-poverty-in-usa.

Fisk, R. P., Anderson, L., Bowen, D. E., Gruber, T., Ostrom, A., Particio, L., . . . Sebastiani, R. (2016). Billions of impoverished people deserve to be better served: A call to action for the service research community. *Journal of Service Management*, *27*(1), 43–55.

Gebauer, H., & Reynoso, J. (2013). An agenda for service research at the base of the pyramid. *Journal of Service Management, 24*(5), 482–502.

Grönroos, C. (1994). From marketing mix to relationship marketing: Towards a paradigm shift in marketing. *Management Decision, 32*(2), 4–20.

Hammond, A., & Prahalad, C.K. (2004). Selling to the poor. *Foreign Policy, 142*(1), 30–37.

Heath, T. P., & Chatzidakis, A. (2012). The transformative potential of marketing from the consumers' point of view. *Journal of Consumer Behavior, 11*(4), 283–291.

Hederman, R., & Rector, R. (2003). The role of parental work in child poverty. Retrieved from The Heritage Foundation website: www.heritage.org/poverty-and-inequality/report/role-parental-work-child-poverty.

Iceland, J., & Hernandez, E. (2017). Understanding trends in concentrated poverty: 1980–2014. *Social Science Research, 62*, 75–95.

Jaiswal, A. K., & Gupta, S. (2015). The influence of marketing on consumption behavior at the bottom of the pyramid. *Journal of Consumer Marketing, 32*(2), 113–124.

Karnani, A. (2007). The mirage of marketing to the bottom of the pyramid: How the private sector can help alleviate poverty. *California Management Review, 49*(4), 90–111.

Mick, D. G. (2006). Presidential address: Meaning and mattering through transformative consumer research. *Advances in Consumer Research, 33*, 1–4.

Mick, D. G., Pettigrew, S., Pechmann, C., & Ozanne, J. L. (2012). *Transformative consumer research for personal and collective well-being.* New York: Routledge.

Miller, Y. (2017, June 14). *Eastern Bank growth fund targets minority-owned firms.* Retrieved from The Bay State Banner website: http://baystatebanner.com/news/2017/jun/14/eastern-bank-growth-fund-targets-minority-owned-fi/?banner-biz.

Minority Business Development Agency. (2017, June 14). *The Minority Business Development Agency: Vital to making America great.* Retrieved from www.mbda.gov/page/minority-business-development-agency-vital-making-america-great.

National Center for Children in Poverty. (2017). *Child poverty.* Retrieved from www.nccp.org/topics/childpoverty.html.

National Women's Law Center. (2016). Child care is fundamental to America's children, families, and economy. Retrieved from https://nwlc.org/wp-content/uploads/2017/01/Child-Care-101-1.17.17.pdf.

Nikulina, V., Widom, C. S., & Czaja, S. (2011). The role of childhood neglect and childhood poverty in predicting mental health, academic achievement and crime in adulthood. *American Journal of Community Psychology, 48*(3–4), 309–321.

Palmatier, R. W. (2008). *Relationship marketing.* Cambridge, MA: Marketing Science Institute. Retrieved from Marketing Sensei: www.mktgsensei.com/AMAE/Services/Relationship%20Marketing.pdf.

Pancer, E., & Handelman, J. (2012). The evolution of consumer well-being. *Journal of Historical Research in Marketing, 4*(1), 177–189.

Prahalad, C. K. (2004). *The fortune at the bottom of the pyramid.* Philadelphia, PA: Wharton School Publishing.

Rogers, R. et al. (2015). The relationship between childhood obesity, low socioeconomic status, and race/ethnicity: Lessons from Massachusetts. *Childhood Obesity, 11*(6), 691–695.

Rojas, C. (2017, May 23). Starbucks' 1st Trenton store to boost minority businesses, train youth. Retrieved from nj.com website: www.nj.com/mercer/index.ssf/2017/05/starbucks_trenton_store_part_of_strategy_to_invest.html.

Rosenbaum, M. C., Corus, C., Ostrom, A., Anderson, L., Fisk, R., Gallan, A., . . . Williams, J. D. (2011). Conceptualization and aspirations of transformative service research. *Journal of Research for Consumers, 19*, 1–6.

Sheth, J., & Sisodia, R. (2012). *The 4 A's of marketing: Creating value for customers, companies and society.* New York: Routledge.

Sirgy, M. J., Lee, D. J., & Rahtz, D. (2007). Research on consumer well-being (CWB): Overview of the field and introduction to the special issue. *Journal of Macromarketing, 27*(4), 341–349.

Starbucks. (2015, July 16). Investing in diverse communities across the U.S. Retrieved from https://news.starbucks.com/news/starbucks-deepens-investments-in-diverse-under-represented-communities.

Stoll, M. A., Raphael, S., & Holzer, H. J. (2004). Black job applicants and the hiring officer's race. *Industrial and Labor Relations Review, 57*(2), 267–287.

UNICEF Office of Research. (2017). *Building the future: Children and the sustainable development goals in rich countries.* Florence, Italy: UNICEF Office of Research.

Weinreich, N. K. (2017). What is social marketing? Retrieved from Weinreich Communications website: www.social-marketing.com/whatis.html.

6   Society and Social Institutions

The Racial, Spatial, and Intergenerational Contours of Food Inequality in America: Origins, Implications, and Conditions of Possibility

Anthony Bayani Rodriguez

To Be Poor and Hungry in One of the Wealthiest Nations in the World

Structural inequality in the early 21st-century United States is experienced in a number of ways, and for upwards of 47 million Americans, the difficulty of obtaining affordable and healthy food is one of them (Feeding America, 2016). In the context of a country recognized as one of the wealthiest on the planet (based on gross domestic product per capita), the challenges faced by poor and low-income individuals and families in accessing vital resources in their neighborhoods (e.g., quality school systems, comprehensive health care, steady employment, livable wages, and community enriching amenities such as recreational parks and green spaces) are issues that are compounded by the adverse health effects of hunger, poor nutrition, and having to choose between inexpensive and unhealthy foods that are easy to obtain versus healthier, more expensive options that are harder to find in areas of concentrated poverty. "Food insecurity" is defined by the chronic lack of access to adequate amounts of affordable, quality, and nutritious food, and in the context of the largest consuming nation on the planet, it is a state of being that exemplifies some of the defining features of the uneven socioeconomic landscape of early 21st-century America.

The rapidly rising cost of fresh and nutritious foods over the past five decades has not been accompanied with proportional improvements in the income of poor and working-class families, or the socioeconomic conditions of the nation's most structurally vulnerable regions, counties, cities, suburbs, and neighborhoods. A 2014 study by the Harvard School of Public Health found that nutritional disparities between America's rich and poor doubled between 2000 and 2010, and while diet quality has improved among people of high socioeconomic status, it has in fact *deteriorated* for low-income populations (Wang et al., 2014). Ultimately, the combination of being poor and living in an area with little or no access to inexpensive and nutritious foods is the double disadvantage that is the basis for the high rates of food insecurity within America's most economically devastated neighborhoods. If food insecurity is largely experienced by low-income families, it nonetheless falls most heavily on the shoulders of single mothers and their children who constitute 36.6% of all children living in food-insecure households (Coleman-Jensen, Rabbit, Gregory, & Singh, 2016). Furthermore, areas in major cities in the United States that are home to predominantly poor and working-class racial and ethnic minorities—namely, African Americans, Latinos, and Native Americans—have the highest rates of *overall* food insecurity and the highest rates of *child* food insecurity in the country compared to predominantly white neighborhoods and higher-income neighborhoods (Emple, 2011; New York Law School Racial Justice Project, 2012; Strings, Ranchod, Laraia, & Nuru-Jeter, 2016).

By and large, studies show that socioeconomic disadvantages are far more determining of chronic hunger and food insecurity than any other factor. Yet, for the disproportionate number of poor and working-class African American, Latino, and Native American families who live with food insecurity, modern racial narratives about biological and cultural predispositions to diet-related diseases continue to circulate not only within these communities themselves, but also in mass media, popular culture, and state discourse regarding the racialized patterns of American public health disparities (Kirkendall, House, & Citro, 2013; New York Law School Racial Justice Project [NYLS-RJP], 2012). Eisenhauer (2001) offers a poignant critique of the political "utility" of approaching health disparities of low-income communities of color as behaviorally or genetically determined despite clear evidence that environmental causes are more influential. Eisenhauer argues:

> [b]y medicalizing the effects of poverty, oppression, abandonment, segregation, and ghettoization, the behavioral/medical approach both reflects and reproduces the existing social order by endorsing an interpretation of health and disease which places responsibility for the pathological effects of these conditions on individuals.
>
> (p. 131)

Disregarding the socioeconomic conditions that make healthy food choices increasingly difficult for people living in areas with low access to fresh and affordable food misdirects scrutiny away from a long history of state-sanctioned regimes of structural inequality that have facilitated and rationalized the unequal distribution of wealth, resources, and political enfranchisement based on ideas of racial, ethnic, and class difference.

This chapter explores the structural origins and spatial politics of contemporary food inequality and its impact on low-income children, parents, and communities that reside among the "food deserts" scattered throughout areas of concentrated poverty throughout the early 21st-century United States. It also examines the ways in which local movements for "food sovereignty" led by the residents of food deserts are confronting the limitations of top-down responses to food insecurity while also introducing alternatives to the profit-driven modern industrial food systems that largely control the planet's food supply.

The Construction of Urban Food Deserts

The relationship of most American consumers to the global food supply is mitigated through multinational corporations and commercial retailers such as grocery stores and restaurants. Along this commodity chain are hundreds and often thousands of miles in which large-scale producers and distributors dominate local economies, creating a situation where masses entrust the quality, affordability, and accessibility of their food supply to a profit-driven industrial economy. Contemporary food inequality is a product of this modern industrial "agri-food system." Since the 1940s, this system has created rapid and exponentially inequitable shifts in the relationships between those who produce, those who consume, and those who profit from the global circulation of both commodities and vital resources like clean water and healthy food. The rise of the modern agri-food system is a result of a combination of factors directly tied to the rapid global expansion of neoliberal paradigms of social governance and financialization that have ensured the steady flow of wealth and resources to the Global North, and the United States in particular. These factors include the disruption of local/regional food economies previously based on local farms, technological advancements and regulatory changes that have magnified the speed, range, and volume by which commodities can be transported, and the rise to dominance of surplus-oriented factory farming techniques and profit-maximizing strategies like monocropping.

The unevenness and instability of the modern food system is the root cause for what Whatmore (2002) describes as "a crisis of *legitimation*," which centers on the politicization of concerns about the consequences of industrialized agriculture for food security, food safety, and the farmed environment at national and local levels (pp. 66–67). Supporting the economic power of multinational corporations are massive investments by the federal government in the food industry so that industrial farming operations can create the most food with the least amount of capital—namely in the form of corn and soy (Segal, 2010). Government agencies such as the Department of Agriculture play a pivotal role in the kinds of food choices that low-income populations have readily available to them. They also play a role in the creation of food deserts by using public funds in ways that disincentivize experimenting with more environmentally sustainable and local models of food production that yield healthier food and boost local economies (Segal, 2010).

One of the primary ways that food inequality has been reproduced over time is in the creation of "food deserts" in areas where large concentrations of poor and systematically under-resourced communities presently reside. Policy makers, government officials, and researchers use the term "food desert" to describe the lack of *affordable* and *convenient* access to healthy produce and food options (NYLS-RJP, 2012). Most recent studies estimate that more than 29 million Americans currently live in food deserts, most of whom live in major metropolitan areas (Ver Ploeg et al., 2012).

The history behind *how* and *why* food deserts exist is linked to both the geopolitical pressures of the industrial agri-food system as well as to state-sanctioned regimes of structural racism that have accumulated over time. Among the decisive causes for the emergence of contemporary *urban* food deserts are the intertwined racial/ethnic and economic transformations of residential spaces (particularly from the 1920s to the 1970s) directly tied to the flight of white middle-class populations to new suburban developments and the coinciding capital disinvestment from areas where largely African American and non-white ethnic minorities dwelled. Although some of the largest cities in the early 21st-century United States show clear patterns of racial segregation, they did not in fact start off this way. The ethnic and economic segregation of America's major metropolitan regions during the 20th century was facilitated by parallel regimes of racially motivated public policy and commercial disinvestment—targeted particularly toward African Americans—which led to cities becoming "racialized repositories of America's poor" (Eisenhauer, 2001, p. 126).

Racially restrictive housing covenants (from the early to mid-20th century), and then mortgage "redlining" policies (from the 1930s to the late 1960s) implemented by the Federal Housing Authority (FHA) and the Veterans Administration (VA), denied and severely limited low-interest home mortgages and loans to residents of certain neighborhoods based exclusively on their racial or ethnic composition rather than on standard measures of creditworthiness (Mahoney, 1995). While the economic mobility and spatial mobility of individuals and families of color living in areas occupied largely by non-whites was stunted (in spite of class), low-interest mortgages were approved for masses of white families and a small number of families of color to purchase homes in new suburban developments. The result was a shift in the racial, ethnic, and class composition of neighborhoods throughout America's major metropolitan regions, which still influences contemporary perceptions about the race and class composition of urban and suburban spaces. This systematic segregation of residential space rooted in ideologies of race and class difference is a key chapter in the 20th-century American history of public and private disinvestment from urban spaces.

Growing Up with Food Insecurity: Toward an Intergenerational Perspective on Solving Food Inequality

Recent estimates project more than 15 million children in the United States live in food-insecure households, and most of these households exist in areas of major cities that have been fundamentally shaped by decades of structural disenfranchisement and neglect. For children and parents alike, food insecurity is directly associated with a wide array of adverse physical and mental health problems. In a 2013 report, Cook identified a number of "nutrition" and "non-nutrition" pathways by which food insecurity impacts the health of children. Cook pointed out that food insecurity's "nutrition pathways" involve the health impacts of the kinds, quality, and amounts of food available, whereas "non-nutrition pathways" are characterized by the health impacts surrounding the stress, distress, worry, and anxiety about managing food insecurity. Food insecurity puts children at risk of compromised health and development from the earliest years of life on through adulthood. The quality and consistency of perinatal and postnatal nutrition of mothers and their babies put infants and children at significant risk of impaired health, emotional and cognitive development, and various other health outcomes that can extend into adulthood (Laraia, Siega-Riz, Gundersen, & Dole, 2006). In the first three to four years of life, food insecurity poses nutritional and non-nutritional health impacts on the development of children's ability to learn, communication skills, interpersonal awareness, self-confidence, trust of parents and supportive adults, and social consciousness (Cook, 2013). Household food insecurity is furthermore associated with psychosocial conditions such as stress, anxiety, and depression, all of which are known to put pregnant mothers and their babies at higher risk of complications and both short and long-term health issues (Laraia et al., 2006).

In addition to what they may or may not be able to eat on a daily basis, the social consciousness of children in low-income households is shaped by the experience of seeing parents choose between preparing healthy meals and maintaining nutritious supplies of food, or paying for other vital expenses such as home rent and bills for home utilities such as electricity and gas (Frank et al., 2006). The stress, distress, worry, and anxiety about where food will come from, what kind of food it will be, and how often it will be replenished is a source of "toxic stress" that is part of children's experience of the non-nutritional impact of food insecurity on health (Cook, 2013). This combination of nutrition and non-nutrition pathways by which food insecurity influences the health of children and their caretakers is associated with a range of adverse health outcomes including increased hospitalizations, diabetes, heart disease, obesity, headaches, gastrointestinal disorders, iron deficiency anemia, aggressiveness/irritability, inattention/hyperactivity, depression, and a range of developmental issues that can drastically impact quality of life in adulthood (Cook, 2013; Laraia et al., 2006; Segal, 2010).

The depth of children's experience of food insecurity and hunger extends beyond what most parental reports, quantitative studies, and medical research suggest. Children are no doubt aware of the food insecurity of their households, and they actively witness and participate in the daily challenges and choices involved in finding meals and adequate food supplies that can sustain their families. As children develop critical awareness of the communities and spaces in which they grow up, they largely draw upon a knowledge reserve composed of ideas and information that their peers and elders share with them and living strategies they acquire from the daily experience of navigating their surroundings. Children's awareness of their social status is shaped by dominant narratives about their neighborhoods, their families, their peers, and ultimately themselves, and children who grow up in food deserts often experience intersecting forms of structural inequality that can play a determining factor in the kinds of opportunities they will have in adulthood. For instance, the widely documented disparity between the funding, curriculum, and environmental quality of schools in low-income areas is only magnified by the impact that food insecurity has on the cognitive development and mental health of children, both of which inhibit their ability to learn at their fullest potential (Jyoti, Frongillo, & Jones, 2005). The nutritional disadvantages of low-income children exacerbate the problems within the actual learning environments of their school systems which typically includes limited access to quality books and literature, large class sizes, standardized-test-based curricula, underqualified teachers, toxic and derelict school buildings, and in some schools, the potential disruptive presence of local police and on-site security officers (NYLS-RJP, 2012). If living in an area that offers little choice but to attend underfunded and under-resourced schools is not already a significant detriment to low-income children's experience of growing up in America, learning to live with poor nutrition, feelings of hunger, and toxic stress in the crucial early years of life is only another burden that can influence their formative perceptions of the degree to which their larger society values their wellbeing and their lives (NYLS-RJP, 2012).

Bringing focused attention to the many ways that food insecurity harms children who grow up in poverty and reside in food deserts is one way of comprehending what it means to live through the present economic disparities, spatial realities, and racial narratives produced by past regimes of inequality. Eradicating food insecurity from the lives of current and future generations of children of low-income neighborhoods requires thinking beyond how to make the modern industrial food system work "better" for the poor. Instead, solutions must be found through sustained efforts to support the creation of food economies that work hand-in-hand with local movements that are changing the terms by which structurally marginalized communities understand their collective capacities to not only disrupt structurally reproduced forms of inequality, but also to introduce alternatives that can transform their neighborhoods into leaders of progressive social change in the 21st century.

The Urgency and Long-Term Limitations of Top-Down Responses to Food Insecurity

Along with other types of businesses, supermarkets followed the flight of white middle-class families to the suburbs beginning in the 1940s and continuing well into the 1980s, even though at a national scale supermarket openings surpassed closings. This gradual disappearance of readily accessible and affordable food retailers within and around spaces of concentrated poverty is a key feature of areas now recognized as urban food deserts (Eisenhauer, 2001; Kirkendall et al., 2013; NYLS-RJP, 2012). For low-income families who live in today's urban food deserts, making healthy choices often means having to buck the additional cost of traveling outside their neighborhoods (more often than not without the use of a car) in order to get to affordable and quality grocery stores. Otherwise, they have no other choice but to rely on local groceries and bodegas that have higher prices, lower inventories, and lower quality produce than the average grocery store in a higher-income neighborhood (Emple, 2011; NYLS-RJP, 2012). Convincing the modern food industry's multinational corporations to participate in creating more low-cost supermarkets in areas of concentrated poverty through government subsidies may offer one solution to the problem of food insecurity in urban food deserts. However, appealing to "big business" to provide better access to low-income consumers is only a partial solution to the broader structural and ideological issues that are to blame for the food inequality experienced by America's poor. The decisions that corporate leaders of the food industry make are largely driven by the forces of global capitalism—an economic system based on ideas about profitability that produce and depend upon unequal, group-differentiated, racialized, classed, gendered, and geographical outcomes. A critical aspect of any long-term strategy to quelling the alarming rates of hunger and food insecurity among America's low-income families must consider more than providing better access to affordable and nutritious food. Such a strategy also must fundamentally change the spatial inequities of the neighborhoods that they call "home" by engaging in serious discussions about creating more affordable housing, local jobs with livable wages, well-funded schools, improved environmental conditions, and supporting efforts to create sustainable local economies that allow residents to claim their rightful stake in creating a healthy future for their children.

Poverty data give strong evidence that implementing national policies to create jobs, raise wages, and expand safety net programs would lead to a drastic and rapid reduction of poverty, and by extension, hunger and food insecurity (Kirkendall et al., 2013). The implementation of such measures nonetheless depends on the adoption of government policies that would make the wealthiest Americans actually pay a share of taxes that is proportional to the exponential income increases they have garnered since the mid-1970s, which are a far cry from the prevailing "trickle-down" policies of the past 50 years that simultaneously *reduce* taxes on the wealthy and *cut* safety nets, job creation programs, and other vital services for the poor and working poor. Until such a progressive shift occurs in the nature of American public policy, there are a number of local and federal state policies that are in place to alleviate hunger and food insecurity in the United States.

More than 47 million Americans, one in seven people, rely on food banks and food stamps provided through the Supplemental Nutrition

Assistance Program (SNAP). It is estimated that upwards of 20 million additional people receive food from food banks, but have never applied for the SNAP program either because their incomes surpass the federal poverty level that would make them eligible for assistance or because they *believe* that they are ineligible for such help (Feeding America, 2016). There are also government policies that promote place-based "community strategies" such as free food giveaways, local business partnerships that ensure healthy and affordable food is available for purchase at nearby groceries, nutrition education programs, offering coupons and SNAP incentives for purchasing healthier foods, and encouraging job creation and training in food production and agricultural skills (Kirkendall et al., 2013). The immediacy and direct assistance provided by these kinds of government food programs make them a critical primary response and a vital lifeline for low-income families. Nevertheless, such top-down responses to food insecurity are not substitutes for more long-term and sustainable strategies that give people the resources to create thriving local food economies within their neighborhoods that lessen dependency on the modern industrial food systems which continually ignore the most structurally vulnerable communities.

The Futurity of Grassroots Food Justice Movements

Local food justice struggles throughout the country are currently offering the most progressive strategies for eradicating food deserts, improving the diets and overall health of children and families within poor neighborhoods, and turning the tide on the perpetuation of racialized, classed, gendered, and *intergenerational* health disparities by prioritizing the voices and long-term needs of local communities (Segal, 2010). New Orleans, New York City, Atlanta, Minneapolis, Detroit, Chicago, Los Angeles, Oakland, San Francisco, Philadelphia, St. Louis, Camden, and Baltimore are among the major cities in the United States where local residents and organizers are leading food justice campaigns in low-income neighborhoods. In the past decade alone, people in these cities have pioneered a grassroots "food sovereignty" model that includes building community-owned and operated gardens within abandoned urban spaces—spaces that city governments actively put up for sale to outside developers who may wish to speculate in projects of "urban renewal," i.e., gentrification. Rather than simply give in to city officials' campaigns and developers' plans to raze city blocks and neighborhoods in order to force low-income families to make way for higher-income populations and commercial ventures, grassroots food justice organizers are taking on the seemingly herculean endeavor of securing land, determining the safety of soils, constructing gardens, and mobilizing community volunteers. Grassroots community-led food sovereignty campaigns are forerunners in the creation of local economies that do not depend on the ebbs and flows of capitalism and do not rely on public policies that often fail to comprehend what local communities need to create sustainable change in their neighborhoods.

The South Bronx in New York City is the poorest congressional district in the country with 37.1% of its residents living below the poverty line (Institute for Children, Poverty, and Homelessness, 2016) and some of the worst health outcomes in the nation. The predominantly African American and Latino population of the South Bronx suffers disproportionately high incidences of obesity, diabetes, asthma, cardiovascular disease, mental illness, and other chronic health conditions, and, as is the case nationwide, they face higher rates of morbidity and mortality compared with white populations from middle-income or wealthier neighborhoods that have the same disease (Pasquel, 2015). South Bronx Unite, a coalition of local residents, organizations, and allies throughout New York City, is presently working together to improve and protect the social, environmental, and economic future of the areas that are home to mostly low-income residents of color (South Bronx Unite, 2017). At present, one of its main campaigns is a legal battle against the encroachment of the grocery delivery company FreshDirect, which is actively seeking a $140 million taxpayer subsidy to place its diesel trucking operation in the South Bronx. According to South Bronx Unite (2017), the Company does not guarantee a single job for local residents, nor does it guarantee that the services offered would be affordable for the families in the area. On the other end of South Bronx Unite's fight against the potential health and environmental impacts of FreshDirect's commercial operations is its leading role in the Mott Haven-Port Morris Land Trust, which formed as a way to identify publicly owned property in the community that was being underused (South Bronx Unite, 2017). Chief among the priorities of this community land trust is the protection of existing community gardens in the South Bronx and the purchase of other places in which new gardens can be constructed.

In Baltimore, Maryland, where one in five people live below poverty level, including nearly a quarter of the city's children five years old and younger, the residents of Sandtown-Winchester are harnessing their collective capacities to gain control and ownership over local spaces, and in turn, provide for each other in ways that public and private entities cannot (Emple, 2011). In the twilight of the Baltimore uprisings of 2015, the Coalition of Friends and the 1619 Coalition, two community organizations in Sandtown-Winchester composed of a small collective of neighborhood residents and local activists, worked together to take over one of the city's 17,000 dilapidated abandoned homes and turn it into a community center they now call "the Harriet Tubman House" (Linderman, 2016). In addition to hosting free clothing giveaways, cultural events, and public forums for discussing local and national political issues, in its first two years of existence the organizers of Tubman House have established three "urban farms" that are feeding the neighborhood's children and adults.

Tubman House's farms are giving community members a space to cultivate cultures of collective agency, mutual aid, and self-sufficiency with political potentials beyond the achievement of food justice. Studies show that the presence of community gardens not only increases the fruit and vegetable consumption of individuals and families who operate and live in proximity to community gardens, but they also have the social effect of reducing rates of crime and even have been shown to have the immediate potential health impact of lowering the blood pressure and stress hormone levels of gardeners themselves (Allen, Alaimo, Elam, & Perry, 2008). These positive health impacts are joined by the invaluable social benefits of nurturing a progressive political consciousness that mobilizes local residents to stake a claim over the health of their community.

One of the founders of Tubman House, Marshall "Eddie" Conway, envisions the larger socially transformative potential of grassroots food justice and food security movements such as those in West Baltimore, the South Bronx, and other low-income neighborhoods throughout the country. In a 2017 interview, he commented:

> [W]hat's most important about all of this is not just the food and the farming, it's the culture and the sense of power it creates for the community. And, it's also about the kids seeing people doing creative and new things in their urban environment . . . Food is always a good starting place for a revolution because you're always going to need three things: food, clothes, and shelter . . . These local movements are really important for protecting these communities' futures, but they are also important in terms of finding out what might work for other communities. I think if we create a local movements on the ground that actually works to change an impoverished neighbourhood into a thriving community, we can set an example that will work for an entire city, and then from there people can do the same thing in other levels, and from there you can influence the regional and national level.
>
> (Rodriguez, 2017, p. 148)

Even if today's local food justice movements do not yet have the means and resources to fully satisfy the needs of everyone in their communities, they are at the forefront of changing how children and adults who live with food insecurity understand the structural origins of their impoverished environments, and the kind of collective effort it will require to change them. As local food sovereignty movements create spaces for adults and children to plant seeds and grow their own food, they are also creating fertile ground for the development of new strategies to survive and potentially move beyond the top-down economic logics of racial capitalism. In doing so, these places are critical landmarks in the 21st-century global geography of social movements "from below" that are *in praxis* transforming the nature of democracy for present and future generations.

References

Allen, J. O., Alaimo, K., Elam, D., & Perry, E. (2008). Growing vegetables and values: Benefits of neighborhood-based community gardens for youth development and nutrition. *Journal of Hunger & Environmental Nutrition, 3*(4), 418–439.

Coleman-Jensen, A., Rabbit, M. P., Gregory, C. A., & Singh, A. (2016). *Household food insecurity in the United States, 2015* (No. 215). Washington, D.C.: USDA. Economic Research Service.

Cook, J. T. (2013, April). Impacts of child food insecurity and hunger on health and development in children: Implications of measurement approach. Presented at the Workshop on Research Gaps and Opportunities on the Causes and Consequence of Child Hunger, Washington, D.C.

Eisenhauer, E. (2001). In poor health: Supermarket redlining and urban nutrition. *GeoJournal, 53*(2), 125–133.

Emple, H. (2011). *Food insecurity among children ages 0–3 in Baltimore City: Barriers to access and initiatives for change.* Baltimore, MD: University of Maryland, Department of Pediatrics.

Feeding America. (2016). 2016 Annual Report. Retrieved from www.feedingamerica. org/about-us/about-feeding-america/annual-report/2016-feeding-america-annual-report.pdf.

Frank, D. A., Neault, N. B., Skalicky, A., Cook, J. T., Wilson, J. D., Levenson, S., . . . Berkowitz, C. (2006). Heat or eat: The low income home energy assistance program and nutritional and health risks among children less than 3 years of age. *Pediatrics, 118*(5), e1293–e1302.

Institute for Children, Poverty, and Homelessness (ICPH). (2016). *Poverty in New York City Council Districts* (On the map: The dynamics of family homelessness in New York City). Retrieved from www.icphusa.org/new_york_city/on-the-map-the-dynamics-of-family-homelessness-in-new-york-city.

Jyoti, D. F., Frongillo, E. A., & Jones, S. J. (2005). Food insecurity affects school children's academic performance, weight gain, and social skills. *The Journal of Nutrition, 135*(12), 2831–2839.

Kirkendall, N. J., House, C. C., & Citro, C. F. (2013). *Research opportunities concerning the causes and consequences of child food insecurity and hunger: Workshop summary.* Washington, D.C.: National Academies Press.

Laraia, B., Siega-Riz, A. M., Gundersen, C., & Dole, N. (2006). Psychosocial factors and socioeconomic indicators are associated with household food insecurity among pregnant women. *Journal of Nutrition, 136*, 177–181.

Linderman, J. (2016, April 22). In vacant Baltimore home, Gray-inspired groups find new life. *AP News.*

Mahoney, M. R. (1995). Segregation, Whiteness, and transformation. *University of Pennsylvania Law Review, 143*(5), 1659–1684.

New York Law School Racial Justice Project (NYLS-RJP). (2012). *NYLS-RJP: How structural racism contributes to the creation and persistence of food deserts (with American Civil Liberties Union)* (Racial Justice Project No. 3). New York.

Pasquel, D. (2015, March 23). Health disparities and environmental justice in the Bronx. Retrieved from https://theejbm.wordpress.com/2015/03/23/health-disparities-and-environmental-justice-in-the-bronx.

Rodriguez, A. B. (2017). Former Black Panther Marshall Eddie Conway on revolutionary political education in the twenty-first century. *The Journal of African American Studies, 21*(1), 138–149.

Segal, A. (2010). Food deserts: A global crisis in New York City. *Consilience: The Journal of Sustainable Development, 3*(1), 197–214.

South Bronx Unite. (2017). Who we are. Retrieved from http://southbronxunite.org.

Strings, S., Ranchod, Y. K., Laraia, B., & Nuru-Jeter, A. (2016). Race and sex differences in the association between food insecurity and Type 2 diabetes. *Ethnicity & Disease, 26*(3), 427–434.

Ver Ploeg, M., Breneman, V., Dutko, P., Williams, R., Snyder, S., Dicken, C., & Kaufman, P. (2012). *USDA ERS: Access to affordable and nutritious food: Updated estimates of distance to supermarkets using 2010 data* (Economic Research Report No. ERR-143). Washington, D.C.: United States Department of Agriculture.

Wang, D. D., Leung, C. W., Li, Y., Ding, E. L., Chiuve, S. E., Hu, F. B., & Willett, W. C. (2014). Trends in dietary quality among adults in the United States, 1999 through 2010. *JAMA Internal Medicine, 174*(10), 1587–1595.

Whatmore, S. (2002). From farming to agribusiness: Global agri-food networks. In R. J. Johnston, P. J. Taylor, & M. J. Watts (Eds.), *Geographies of global change* (2nd ed., pp. 57–67). Malden, MA: Blackwell.

7   History

The Evolution of Juvenile Justice

Harold T. Broderick

Introduction

The legal system has historically treated children as chattel with few if any rights or legal protections. The idea of developing a separate standard and status for children was given little thought throughout much of legal history. Children had virtually no rights until roughly the mid-20th century. When accused of a crime, they were subjected to the same system of sanctions and punishment applied to adults. There were no juvenile courts, and nor were there any criminal laws or statutes that considered the special status of youngsters. Children who, through fate or circumstance, were deemed runaway, delinquent, or neglected, were dealt with in the same manner and with equal harshness as adults. No specific facilities existed to address status offenses or very minor infractions, and children not guilty of any crime were often placed in community asylums or homes for wayward children. Those unfortunate enough to be charged and convicted of more significant offenses were subjected to the same sentences and punishment as adults.

A significant turning point in the nascent development of the welfare of children occurred with the advent of urbanization and industrialization. Slowly but inexorably, society became increasingly concerned about the myriad issues regarding children. The initial response to these concerns resulted in the child-saving movement, groups of people who advocated for the rights and welfare of children. These groups represented the first significant efforts to definitively establish children as a distinct and separate class with unique problems emanating primarily from their age and socio-economic situation. Many people involved in these movements belonged to a higher social class and economic status. They viewed certain categories of children as not only morally susceptible to negative influences but also as a group that should be monitored, directed, and controlled by social, legislative, and other agencies. These agencies, mostly governmental in nature, were, in turn, responsive to the substantial influence of prominent, socially active, and powerful groups. An overriding and constant factor in this rapidly growing, challenging, and constantly evolving field was the issue of poverty.

Origins of America's Juvenile Justice System

To understand the evolution and current status of our juvenile justice system, it is essential to consider where the foundation of our structure of juvenile jurisprudence originated. Laws regarding children in the early years of the nation were heavily influenced by the common law of England. Therefore, some of the earliest laws relating to children in the United States can be found in English Poor Laws (Quigley, 1996). These laws, first passed by Parliament in 1535, coincided with the rise of the apprenticeship movement and the chancery courts, each of which had a significant impact on the developing system of justice pertaining to juveniles.

The Poor Laws created a system of overseers empowered to identify, regulate, and manage children who were neglected, truant, impoverished, or had no permanent place of residence. They focused on children who belonged to what was considered an inferior class within the broader community. The legal rights and protection of children were virtually non-existent. Children over the age of five were considered small adults with the same responsibilities and work obligations as their adult counterparts. The Elizabethan Poor Laws of 1601 expanded this system, adding church wardens who, with the overseers, exercised considerable influence on the developing system of juvenile justice. They had the authority of the king to place poor or orphaned children in involuntary apprenticeships, workhouses, or almshouses (Rendleman, 1971). Conditions in these institutions were often harsh and abusive. Children were unable to learn trades and were simultaneously in close proximity to adults of questionable character, often with criminal histories.

Guided by the principle of *parens patriae*, meaning "parent of the nation," chancery courts in England and Wales exercised their jurisdiction over issues involving property, inheritance rights, and the welfare of orphans. Thus, the courts also had the right to place children in involuntary apprenticeships. Apprenticeships were already a well-established practice in England (Rendleman, 1971). Once placed, children were to be trained by a tradesman or "master" in a specific profession until they came of age (usually 21). In exchange for their labor, children were to receive food, shelter, and clothing. However, there was no regulatory oversight or supervision (National Voice of Foster Parents, 2016). Often subjected to harsh and physically demanding conditions, children were viewed as a form of property or chattel with no legal protection or personal rights. These attitudes prevailed whether the children were orphans or natural-born children of the home. Stubborn Child laws were passed in the Massachusetts Bay Colony in 1646 requiring children to obey their parents, and moral discipline was rigidly enforced (Sutton, 1988). Seven-year-old children in Massachusetts in 1648 could legally be put to death for cursing at their parents (Bueche, 1999). Thus, these were beliefs also held by the Colonists.

Significant changes regarding the legal status of children finally began to emerge during the 1700s. Sir William Blackstone, one of England's most prominent lawyers, was among the first to legally define children's rights. Defying the concept of children as chattel, he outlined three duties parents owed to their children: maintenance, protection, and education (Blackstone, 1893). In his *Commentaries on the Laws of England* published in the 1760s, Blackstone also identified two things required to hold a person accountable for a crime. These were, first, a vicious will and, second, the committing of an unlawful act. The first of these requirements made it possible to define "infants" as exempt from conviction because they were incapable of holding a vicious will. "Under seven years of age indeed an infant cannot be guilty of felony; for then a felonious discretion is almost an impossibility in nature; but at eight years old he may be guilty of felony" (Blackstone, 1893, 4:2). A felony refers to any kind of serious crime such as burglary, assault, kidnapping, or murder. Within his explanatory text, Blackstone made the case that children 14 and older are generally capable of having a vicious will, but children between the ages of 7 and 14 would need to be decided on a case-by-case basis as this was when the capacity for vicious will developed. One child might be quite cunning at age 9 while another child doesn't reach the same level of thought until age 13. Children could be tried for a major crime if it could be proven that they had the capacity to discern right from wrong. For example, a 10-year-old boy was convicted of murder and sentenced to death when it was proved that he tried to hide the body, indicating he recognized guilt (Blackstone, 1893). Building from this work, Thomas Spence published *Rights of Infants* in 1796, one of the earliest assertions of the rights of children in English law.

American Principles Emerge

The advent of a juvenile justice system in the newly independent United States continued to incorporate many of the common law practices established in England. The patriarchal family unit remained the core of the community as well as the primary source of social control. Despite some progress in the developing rights of children, by the mid-1800s, children were still commonly treated as chattel, particularly poor children. Whether in the home of their birth or if placed in homes as voluntary or involuntary indentured servants, by 1850 there remained no laws protecting children from harm at the hands of their purported caretakers (Markel, 2009). Parents and those charged with the care of children had complete and virtually unchallenged authority to discipline children as they deemed necessary. Children could be treated with extreme cruelty at home, at school, and by the law as they were subjected to corporal punishment, prison, or even the death penalty (Newman, 1978). It was a time when people fully believed in the maxim, "spare the rod and spoil the child." Even in cases where punishment resulted in death, there were few cases in which the parents were tried for murder. Without any legal rights of their own, children and those concerned with their welfare had few available options.

Renewed interest in these issues emerged in the first half of the 19th century. Increased immigration and the resultant population growth, combined with increased migration to the cities during the Industrial Revolution, brought this relatively dormant subject to a newly concerned citizenry. This renewed interest in the plight of poor children gave rise to several groups of socially prominent activists and reformers who were referred to as the child savers, a movement that began in New York City. The Society for the Prevention of Juvenile Delinquency was formed in the 1820s specifically to address the problem of children being incarcerated with adults. This practice tended to place children into early, and often permanent, interaction with adult experts in crime (Philanthropy Roundtable, 2017). Arguing that young people needed their own system of adjudication, counseling, and incarceration, these social activists founded the first House of Refuge in New York City in 1825 (Fox, 1970). As a privately managed facility, the group home accepted young people who had already been in trouble with the legal system as well as children who, in the opinion of the child savers, were impoverished or otherwise deemed to be on a path to delinquency. The creation of the House of Refuge brought significant attention to the vast numbers of children found abandoned, orphaned, abused, or neglected within New York's slums. On their own, these children had little choice but to beg, engage in prostitution, become petty thieves, or join gangs. Following the basic mandates of the House of Refuge, other institutions opened in Westboro, Massachusetts in 1848 and in Rochester, New York in 1849 (U.S. Department of Justice, 1976). Other states soon followed and, by 1900, 36 states had juvenile reform schools (Sutton, 1988).

Yet, there was still little concern for the rights of the children themselves. The admissions standards of these houses of refuge reflected this. Many of the children confined were not guilty of any criminal offense, but were instead status offenders (i.e., juveniles who engage in behavior which would not be criminal if they were adults) or simply homeless. The facilities were managed in a rigid manner with strict rules for the children. The daily regimen was semi-military in nature. All activities from sleeping to eating to exercise and training took place at a specified time and place. The children lived in a prison-like atmosphere with severe punishment for any violation of the rules and regulations. They engaged in supervised labor, basic education, and weekly religious activities. Upon reaching a certain level of assessed reformation, children could be bound into apprenticeships with outside employers. The employers would continue to supervise and care for them for a specified period after which it was expected that the children, now adults, would be fully rehabilitated and able to support themselves (Philanthropy Roundtable, 2017).

Among the many efforts to address these complex issues was one made by philanthropist Charles Loring Brace, a graduate of Yale College. In 1853, Brace founded the Children's Aid Society in New York City (Fox, 1970).

Brace believed that the approach taken by the larger institutions was insufficient to help vulnerable children develop into strong adults. While he thought that work and education were important components of childhood, he also believed that a strong family environment was an essential element of a solid and stable foundation. Brace concluded there were too many children of need in New York City to be adequately cared for. He was also aware that families in western farming communities could provide homes and care for many of these children. With that in mind, Brace devised what he referred to as his "placing out plan" which became known as the Orphan Train movement. These orphan trains made prearranged stops in various farming communities where prospective adoptive families would meet the children and "adopt" them on the spot. In this manner, more than 150,000 children were relocated to families in the West between the years of 1853 and 1929 (Aspiration, Acculturation, and Impact, 2017).

Renewed Focus on Justice for Juveniles

The Orphan Train movement is perhaps the preeminent illustration of the complex and seemingly insoluble issue of how to address the needs of unfortunate children. Countless programs and initiatives over the course of decades sought to protect the welfare of children; however, there still were no constitutional protections assuring the rights of children. This reality was starkly demonstrated in the 1874 case of Mary Ellen McCormack. At the age of two, Mary Ellen was placed with foster parents, Francis and Mary Connolly, who lived in a New York City tenement. Mary Ellen's father was killed during the Civil War, leaving her mother destitute and unable to provide for her. "Momma has been in the habit of whipping and beating me almost every day," the little girl testified regarding her foster mother. "She used to whip me with a twisted whip" (Markel, 2009). Despite the obvious physical and emotional harm, those who wished to protect the little girl had difficulty finding a legal basis on which to proceed. In desperation, they turned to the Society for the Prevention of Cruelty to Animals. While there was no specific law to protect children from abuse, there were laws protecting animals. Learning of the case, it was observed animals had greater rights than children (Markel, 2009). The case was heard by the New York State Supreme Court and Mary Ellen was placed in an orphanage (Hockenberry & Puzzenchera, 2014). In response to this case, the New York Society for the Prevention of Cruelty to Children was formed in 1874 (Markel, 2009). The first child protective agency in the world, the organization still works to bring new and innovative programs forward to provide counseling, legal, and educational services to abused and neglected children.

With the founding of these organizations, social activists concerned with the plight of children were becoming increasingly influential across the country. In 1889 Jane Addams of Chicago founded Hull House which conducted research toward improving the condition of children. For example, Addams and her colleagues studied the role of leisure in the health of youth and the role of human services in advocating for the needs of children. Their efforts contributed to the establishment of the first juvenile court in the United States. This watershed event occurred on July 1, 1899 when the city of Chicago passed the Illinois Juvenile Court Act. This court, located in Cook County, created the first bifurcated legal system with a discrete juvenile court for those under the age of 16. By 1912, 22 states had copied Illinois's legislation and by 1925, every state except two had followed suit (Krisbeg & Austin, 1993).

From Chattel to Children

The Chicago juvenile court system was predicated on the principles of reformation and rehabilitation rather than the prior dictate of punishment. The doctrine of *parens patriae* was an underlying principle upon which the court relied. This principle extended the power of the state to act in an intrusive manner upon families when children were involved. For the first time in jurisprudence, children were recognized as a separate and distinct class of citizenry. The court viewed children as needing guidance, support, and encouragement. This benevolent view was intended to supply children with the means to live a lawful and productive life as part of the larger community. Within two years of the court's founding, Jane Addams founded the Juvenile Protective Association (JPA), through which the first juvenile probation officers were appointed—a responsibility eventually assumed by the government (Juvenile Protective Association, 2007). In addition to advocating for children's rights, the JPA conducts research into racism, exploitation of children, child labor issues, drug abuse, and child prostitution. Their purpose is to understand how these aspects of society affect child development and how this information might improve conditions for vulnerable children or mitigate damage already created (Juvenile Protective Association, 2007). It also works to influence policy and advocate for children's rights.

The early juvenile courts adopted the goals of the reform schools in that their focus was on reforming children into productive adults rather than punishing them. Again looking to the legal doctrine of *parens patriae*, a new perspective emerged regarding the appropriate way to raise a child. No longer was the overriding doctrine one of "spare the rod, spoil the child." Now there was a focus on what was "in the best interests of the child." To that end, cases were tried as civil or noncriminal actions and there was a significant reduction in the number of procedural rules. This was meant to reinforce a less adversarial atmosphere. The hope was that juvenile offenders would be encouraged to take a more responsible, law-abiding approach in the future if they were treated in a fair and equitable manner. The court had significant discretion in adjudicating their cases. Judge Julian Mack, one of the first judges of the Cook County Juvenile Court, described the court's character in this way:

> The child who must be brought into court should, of course, be made to know that he is face to face with the power of the state, but he should . . . be made to feel that he is the object of its care and solicitude . . . Seated at a desk, with the child at his side, where he can on occasion put his arm around his shoulder and draw the lad to him, the judge, while losing none of his judicial dignity, will gain immensely in the effectiveness of his work.
>
> (Mack, 1909, p. 120)

When necessary, juvenile courts retained the power to order the removal of young offenders from their homes to be housed in juvenile reform institutions or in the developing system of foster care services. Over the next six decades, social activists, politicians, legal scholars, and a citizenry whose interest ranged from indifference to outrage all put forth proposals, thoughts, and opinions on how to effectively address children in need across a broad spectrum of social and legal issues. Constitutional due process rights afforded to adults, however, were systematically denied to juveniles. Although transformational changes to children's rights laws would not take place for another 60 years, when instituted, they would revolutionize the legal parameters of the juvenile system of jurisprudence and set a precedent for its future administration.

A New Era in Children's Rights?

Although the creation of the first juvenile court in 1899 indicated movement toward greater protections and rights for children, few changes occurred during the first half of the 20th century. Children continued to have limited legal protection in favor of parental rights or, increasingly, courtroom determinations. It wasn't until 1935 and President Roosevelt's New Deal legislation that the federal government focused on child welfare and intervention. The Social Security Act authorized the Children's Bureau "to cooperate with state public-welfare agencies in establishing, extending, and strengthening, especially in predominantly rural areas, [child welfare services] for the protection and care of homeless, dependent, and neglected children, and children in danger of becoming delinquent" (Social Security Act, 1935). This enabled juvenile courts to intervene more fully in children's cases when it was believed children could be redirected toward a positive life path by removing them from impoverished homes and placing them in collective rehabilitation centers. Concerns grew, however, as disparities in the adjudication of justice emerged. This was due to the subjective and arbitrary rulings of judges.

"Similarly situated youths could receive vastly different sentences based on the mood, temperament, or personal philosophy of individual judges" (Center on Juvenile and Criminal Justice, 2017). This also meant children from homes with greater poverty could expect to be remanded to group institutions faster than children from families of middle or higher income.

These issues began to be addressed during the turbulent 1960s when political and social unrest permeated and divided the country. It was during this period that a series of precedent-setting Supreme Court decisions pertaining to the due process rights of children forever changed the administration of the juvenile justice system. Due process first emerged in the Magna Carta of 1215 when King John of England declared,

> No free man shall be seized or imprisoned, or stripped of his rights or possessions, or outlawed or exiled, or deprived of his standing in any other way, nor will we proceed with force against him, or send others to do so, except by the lawful judgment of his equals or by the law of the land.
>
> (Davis, 1989)

Due process clauses are found in the Fifth and Fourteenth Amendments providing safeguards against arbitrary denial of life, liberty, or property by the government outside the sanction of the law (Madison, 2010). The Fifth Amendment's due process clause applies to the conduct of the federal government while the Fourteenth Amendment limits the power of states to deny due process or equal protection to its citizens. Constitutional protections within the juvenile court system were considered unnecessary and viewed by some as a hindrance that would interfere with the court's mission.

Establishment of Juvenile Due Process Rights

The first major decision affecting the rights of children was *Kent v. United States* (1966). This case involved the waiver of jurisdiction from a juvenile to an adult court. Morris Kent entered the juvenile court system of the District of Columbia as a 14-year-old charged with several burglaries and an attempted purse snatching. At the age of 16 and while on probation, he was charged with housebreaking, robbery, and rape based on fingerprints found at the crime scene. After being taken into custody and interrogated by police, Kent confessed to this as well as other criminal acts. The juvenile court had exclusive jurisdiction over his case, but it also had the right to transfer the defendant to an adult court "after full investigation." Although a psychiatric evaluation indicated Kent suffered from severe psychopathology and doctors recommended he be placed in a psychiatric hospital, the juvenile court waived its jurisdiction, elevating the case to an adult criminal U.S. District Court. Indicted by a grand jury, Kent was convicted and sentenced to 30 to 90 years in prison.

A series of appeals led to the case being heard by the Supreme Court. In their majority decision authored by Justice Abe Fortas, the Court found the procedures followed by the juvenile court were inadequate. For a waiver to be valid, the Court ruled the following conditions must be present: (1) A hearing must be held on the motion of waiver, (2) the child is entitled to be represented by counsel, (3) the defense attorney must be given access to all records and reports relied upon to reach a waiver decision, and (4) the court must provide a written statement of the reasons for the waiver. Because none of these conditions had been met, the waiver of jurisdiction was determined invalid. In this decision, Justice Fortas stated: "There may be grounds for concern that the child receives the worst of both worlds [in juvenile courts], that he gets neither the protection accorded to adults nor the solicitous care and regenerative treatment postulated for children" (*Kent v. United States*, 1966). The court expressed the view that the principles of *parens patriae* was not realized. Kent was denied the constitutional due process rights given adults while also deprived of the rehabilitation implied under juvenile law.

One year later, the Supreme Court ruled on the case of Gerald Gault (*In re Gault*, 1967). This case is considered the leading constitutional case in juvenile law. Gerald Gault was 15 when he was accused of making obscene phone calls to a neighbor in his home state of Arizona. At the time, Gault was serving a six-month probationary period for being present when another boy stole a woman's wallet. Gault was arrested at his home while his parents were at work. The following day, a hearing was held before a juvenile judge in chambers. Present were the defendant, his mother, his older brother, and two probation officers. The complainant was not present, no witnesses were present, no sworn testimony was taken, no transcript or written record was kept, and there was no documentation of the substance of the proceedings. In fact, information regarding this proceeding was derived primarily from the testimony of the judge given at a subsequent habeas corpus hearing.

Gault was committed to the state's Industrial School for a period of six years, "for the period of his minority (that is, until 21), unless sooner discharged by due process of law" (*In re: Gault*, 1967). A similar offense committed by an adult would have a maximum fine of $50 and a possible sentence not to exceed two months' confinement. The Supreme Court delivered a complex and expansive decision reversing the judgment of the Arizona Supreme Court and remanding the case. Writing for the majority, Justice Fortas wrote, "neither the Fourteenth Amendment nor the Bill of Rights is for adults alone" (*In re: Gault*, 1967). Justice Douglas wrote, "Neither man nor child can be allowed to stand condemned by methods which flout constitutional requirements of due process of law" (*In re Gault*, 1967). Justice Potter, in his dissent, argued requiring the application of certain due process procedures to the juvenile sector would have the unwanted effect of converting juvenile cases into criminal cases. This could circumvent the principle of *parens patriae* and return juvenile law to the adversarial procedures of the past, when children were tried based on adult judicial standards.

The Kent and Gault cases addressed due process in juvenile waiver and adjudication hearings respectively. The Court continued to move toward providing due process rights to children with their decision in the case of *In re Winship* (1970). This case involved a 12-year-old boy charged with theft of more than $100 from a woman's purse. The standard of proof for a conviction in juvenile court was "a preponderance of the evidence." This is a lower standard of proof sufficient to find a defendant guilty in adult civil court proceedings, but not criminal proceedings where "beyond a reasonable doubt" standards are applied. This higher standard is applicable when the accused is facing incarceration if convicted. In the Winship case, the child was facing the possibility of six years in a juvenile training center for "the best interest of the child," providing care, protection, and rehabilitation. The Court rejected this logic, stating that "good intentions do not themselves obviate the need for criminal due process safeguards in juvenile courts" (*In re Winship*, 1970), particularly when the child's loss of liberty is at stake. The Court ruled that the higher standard of "beyond a reasonable doubt" must apply to minors in the same manner as it is applied in adult criminal courts. Both Chief Justice Burger and Justice Potter dissented from the majority opinion. They argued the application of adult criminal court procedures to the juvenile courts was moving away from the basic tenets of the juvenile court and contrary to its original purpose. Burger wrote, "I cannot regard it as a manifestation of progress to transform juvenile courts into criminal courts, which is what we are well on the way to accomplishing" (*In re Winship*, 1970). This statement reflected a significant concern of those involved in the increasingly controversial and complex decisions that emanated from juvenile court proceedings.

Perhaps with this in mind, the Court took a step back in the case of *McKeiver v. Pennsylvania* (1971). Joseph McKeiver and Edward Terry, both 16, were charged with robbery, assault, and escape. Their request to the juvenile court of Philadelphia for a jury trial was denied. This decision was affirmed by both the Superior and Supreme Courts of Pennsylvania. In its ruling, the Supreme Court was clearly concerned that the inclusion of a jury trial in the juvenile court system would bring it closer to the adult adversarial court system and change the informal nature that was essential to the idealistic process and success of the juvenile system. In its decision, announced by Justice Blackmun, the Court cited both the Sixth and Fourteenth Amendments, ruling that a jury trial is not constitutionally required in a juvenile court's adjudicative stage, but could be an issue to be decided by each state in turn.

If the formalities of criminal adjudicative process are to be superimposed on the juvenile court system, there is no need for its separate existence. Perhaps the ultimate disillusionment will come one day, but for the moment we are disinclined to give impetus to it.

(McKeiver v. Pennsylvania, 1971)

The Court acknowledged juvenile courts had not been allotted sufficient resources necessary to comprehensively address the issues of young offenders. However, the Court was "reluctant to disallow the states to experiment further and to seek in new and different ways the elusive answers to the problems of the young" (*McKeiver v. Pennsylvania*, 1971). Three Justices joined in the dissent, arguing:

> Where a state uses its juvenile court proceedings to prosecute a juvenile for a criminal act and to order confinement until the juvenile reaches 21 years of age . . . then [the juvenile] is entitled to the same procedural protection as an adult.

(McKeiver v. Pennsylvania, 1971)

Juvenile Justice Venue

These series of decisions applied many established case law standards present in the adult system to the juvenile justice system. The application of constitutional protections extended to juveniles was, in some cases, straightforward and clear while the dissents indicate there was also a blurring of the traditional separation, purpose, and distinctions of this bifurcated system. The California case of *Breed v. Jones* (1975) may be viewed as an attempt by the Court to re-establish a clear delineation between adult and juvenile cases. At the age of 17, Gary Jones was charged with armed robbery. His case was adjudicated in juvenile court and he was found guilty by a judge. The judge then transferred the case to the adult criminal court where a second trial concluded with a conviction. Defense attorneys argued the transfer and subsequent conviction violated the double jeopardy clause outlined in the Fifth Amendment.

Prior to this case, double jeopardy had only been applied in adult criminal court cases. The lower courts ruled the double jeopardy clause did not apply since adjudication at the juvenile court level was distinctly different from its adult counterpart. The Supreme Court reversed this ruling. Justice Burger delivered the opinion of the Court, holding that the prosecution of the respondent in Superior Court violated the double jeopardy clause of the Fifth Amendment as applied through the Fourteenth Amendment. The adult conviction was ordered vacated and the case remanded to the California Court of Appeals for disposition. This case prohibits the waiver of a case from a juvenile to an adult court for trial once a prior adjudicatory hearing has been held. The state must first decide if a child will be prosecuted in the juvenile system or waived to an adult court. Once the venue is established, the case must proceed in the chosen forum, thus ensuring the child's due process rights.

Poverty and Juvenile Justice

A common theme evident in the rulings of the Supreme Court throughout this period was the acknowledgment that the juvenile justice system lacked the resources necessary to effectively address the enormous responsibility of its mission, problems that persist today. The inherent inequity of the system places the poor and disenfranchised at a distinct disadvantage. Without adequate resources, the ultimate result is often directly related to the representation one can afford. These cases also highlight the degree to which the courts allow for subjectivity from one state to another. A disturbing trend within the system has been the over-representation of minorities and poverty-stricken children within the legal system. Rather than having a clear, consistent legal code that applies to all juveniles throughout the country, juvenile laws differ significantly from state to state and even county to county. This includes the age at which children charged criminally can be tried as adults. Juvenile jurisdiction is defined by State Statute and is defined as the oldest age at which a juvenile court can exercise jurisdiction. Four states set this age at 15, 10 states at 16, and the majority of states at 17. Some states exercise concurrent jurisdiction where prosecutors have discretion to bring charges in either juvenile or adult court based on the age, offense, and prior record of the juvenile (Office of Justice Programs, 2012).

Even the issue of the minimum age at which persons convicted of murder could receive the death penalty was not resolved until 1975, when the Court ruled that no person under the age of 18 at the time of commission of a capital offense may be sentenced to death (*Roper v. Simmons*, 2005). Because juvenile cases are not uniformly reported across the country due to the vast array of "remedies" within the system, it is difficult to ascertain with specificity the role poverty plays in the overall judicial procedures of the juvenile courts. According to McCord, Spatz-Widom, and Crowell (2001), black youth between the ages of 10 and 17 represented only 15 percent of the U.S. population in 1997, but

> 26 percent of all juvenile arrests, 30 percent of delinquency referrals to juvenile courts, 45 percent of all pre-adjudication decisions, 33 percent of petitioned delinquency cases, 46 percent of cases judicially waived to adult criminal court, and 40 percent of juveniles in public long-term institutions.
>
> (p. 231)

Hispanic and American Indian juveniles are also overrepresented in the juvenile and adult justice systems. The inference is unambiguously clear. Inequality continues to exist within our system of juvenile jurisprudence. Juveniles face the dual inequity of the disparate application of the law as well as the intrinsic nature of a system where the poor and disadvantaged are clearly overrepresented. While remaining complex, confusing, and often inconsistent, the evolution of juvenile justice is moving in a positive direction. The unbiased and equitable application of our Constitution as mandated by Supreme Court rulings still engenders optimism and confidence for the future of our juvenile justice system.

References

Aspiration, Acculturation, and Impact: Immigration to the United States, 1789–1930. (2017). The Children's Aid Society. Retrieved from http://ocp.hul.harvard.edu/immigration/cas.html.

Blackstone, W. (1893). *Commentaries on the Laws of England in Four Books*. Philadelphia, PA: J.B. Lippincott Co.

Breed v. Jones, 421 U.S. 519 (1975).

Bueche, J. (1999). U.S. History. *State of Louisiana*. Retrieved from http://ojj.la.gov/index.php?page=sub&id=230.

Center on Juvenile and Criminal Justice. (2017). Juvenile Justice History. Retrieved from www.cjcj.org/education1/juvenile-justice-history.html.

Davis, G. R. C. (1989). *Magna Carta*. Revised Edition. London: British Library Publications.

Fox, S. J. (1970). Juvenile Justice Reform: A Historical Perspective. *Stanford Law Review* 22: 1187.

Hockenberry, S., & Puzzenchera, C. (2014). *Delinquency Cases in Juvenile Court*. Washington D.C.: National Center for Juvenile Justice.

In re Gault, 387 U.S.1 (1967).

In re Winship, 397 U.S. 358 (1970).

Juvenile Protective Association. (2007). Mission and Vision. Retrieved from http://jpachicago.org/about.

Kent v. United States, 383 U.S. 541 (1966).

Krisberg, B., & Austin, J. (1993). *Reinventing Juvenile Justice*. Newbury Park, CA: Sage Publications.

Mack, J. (1909). The Juvenile Court. *Harvard Law Review* 23: 104–122.

Madison, P. A. (2010, August 2). Historical Analysis of the Meaning of the 14th Amendment's First Section. *The Federalist Blog*. Retrieved from www.federalistblog.us/mt/articles/14th_dummy_guide.htm#due.

Markel, H. (2009, December 14). Case Shined First Light on Abuse of Children. *The New York Times*. Retrieved from www.nytimes.com/2009/12/15/health/15abus.html.

McCord, J., Spatz-Widom, C., & Crowell, N. A. (2001). *Juvenile Crime, Juvenile Justice*. Washington D.C.: National Academy Press.

McKeiver v. Pennsylvania, 403 U.S. 528 (1971).

National Voice of Foster Parents. (2016). History of Foster Care. Retrieved from http://nfpaonline.org/page-1105741.

Newman, G. (1978). *The Punishment Response*. Philadelphia, PA: Lippincott.

Office of Justice Programs. (2012). *Statistical Briefing Book*. Washington D.C.: Office of Juvenile Justice and Delinquency Prevention.

Philanthropy Roundtable. (2017). 1825: A Refuge for Juvenile Delinquents. Retrieved from www.philanthropyroundtable.org/almanac/economic_and_social_prosperity/1825_a_refuge_for_juvenile_delinquents.

Quigley, W. P. (1996). Five Hundred Years of English Poor Laws, 1349–1834: Regulating the Working and Nonworking Poor. *Akron Law Review* 30: 73–128.

Rendleman, D. R. (1971). *Porens Patriae*: From Chancery to the Juvenile Court. *South Carolina Law Review* 23: 205.

Roper v. Simmons, 543 U.S. 551 (2005).

Social Security Act. (1935). § 521, 49 Stat. 620, 633.

Sutton, J. R. (1988). Stubborn Children: Controlling Delinquency in the United States, 1640–1981. Berkeley, CA: University of California Press.

U.S. Department of Justice. (1976). Juvenile Justice and Delinquency Prevention, Two Hundred Years of American Criminal Justice: An LEAA Bicentennial Study. Washington, D.C.: Law Enforcement Assistance Administration.

8 The Arts

Arts Education and Makerspaces: Opportunities for Democratizing Practices and Supporting Socially Responsible Learning

Sandra Schamroth Abrams

Overview

Arts education is important to the development of abilities and understandings, including but not limited to critical thinking (Bowen, Greene, & Kisida, 2014); academic achievement (Catterall, 2009); imagination, interpretation, and agency (Davis, 2008); positive emotional responses (Brown & Sax, 2013); and an appreciation for the arts (Parsad, Spiegelman, & Coopersmith, 2012). The acts of creating, questioning, and interacting have "humanizing" components that can promote educational equity and the democratization and destabilization of normative discourse and policies (Chappell & Cahnmann-Taylor, 2013). Though a causal relationship between arts education and cognitive transfer may be difficult to prove, there are other areas of causality that a review of research has suggested: drama and reading readiness; classical music and spatial thinking; and musical experimentation and spatial thinking (Hetland, Winner, Veenema, & Sheridan, 2013). Despite these and other established benefits, arts education, integration, and development have been superseded by an assessment culture that honors standardized tests, rote learning, and contrived answers.

Movements to foster arts education have revealed concerted efforts to support youth engagement. The national Turnaround Arts school program, which was founded in 2011 and is sponsored by the John F. Kennedy Center for the Performing Arts, the President's Committee on the Arts and Humanities, the U.S. Department of Education, the National Endowment for the Arts, as well as private and local partners (About us, n.d.), provides arts education programs to the lowest-performing schools in 17 states and Washington, D.C. In addition to offering schools necessary supplies, the program hinges on the partnership of art specialists and established artists with particular schools, fostering a learning community that supports the integration of arts instruction and performance. Pilot research reveals that, between 2011 and 2014, students in the Turnaround Arts schools exhibited a 22.55% gain in math proficiency and a 12.62% gain in reading proficiency (Impact, n.d.).

Despite efforts and results such as these, arts education does not receive enough time and attention, especially for those who live in low-income areas.

Since the passage of No Child Left Behind, which strengthened the culture of accountability, support for arts education has waned (Hetland, Winner, Veenema, & Sheridan, 2013). Research (Kraehe, Acuff, & Travis, 2016) further reveals that the lack of support for the arts may have the most dramatic effects on those from low-income areas given that "arts educational resources are withheld from students attending schools with high concentrations of racial minorities and students living in poverty" (p. 237). Furthermore, there is limited arts education in early childhood settings in disadvantaged areas (Brown & Sax, 2013, p. 339) even though research indicates that children in low-income areas benefitted from attending "arts-rich" schools (Catterall, 2009). In other words, there are disparities in education, and the arts need to be central, not peripheral, to the conversation, especially for children in impoverished neighborhoods and schools.

Childhood Arts Education: Research and Concerns

In 2012, the National Center for Education Statistics (NCES) published survey data related to elementary music, visual arts, and classroom arts instruction within a 10-year span (1999–2000 and 2009–2010). The report's opening sentence underscores the overarching issue addressed in this edited collection in general, and this chapter in particular: "Student access to arts education and the quality of such instruction in the nation's public schools continue to be of concern to policymakers, educators, and families" (Parsad, Spiegelman, & Coopersmith, 2012, p. 1). Rightfully so, as research reveals that, around the 1990s, early childhood arts education began seeing a downturn, and there were negative cascading effects for those from historically marginalized populations. Though "the decline of childhood arts education among white children is relatively insignificant . . . the declines for African American and Hispanic children are quite substantial—49% for African American and 40% for Hispanic children" (Rabkin & Hedberg, 2011, p. 15). And, given that research suggests that youth who experience sustained engagement with the arts have a greater chance of attending and graduating college, becoming actively involved in the community, voting in elections, and maintaining a full-time job (Catterall, 2009; Rabkin & Hedberg, 2011), the absence of arts education among those in low-income areas potentially creates and/or perpetuates long-lasting inequities. It comes as no surprise, therefore, that those in poverty continue to be disempowered by the absence of robust arts education (Wexler, 2014) and the "continuing marginalization of the arts in education" has become a common understanding among many education researchers (Glass, Meyer, & Rose, 2013).

Though the NCES survey suggested that music education seems to have maintained a foothold between 2000 and 2010, other forms of art, such as dance, drama, and visual arts, saw a decline. In 2010, of the elementary schools surveyed about their weekly arts instruction, 93% offered music instruction, 85% offered visual arts instruction, 58% offered drama/

theatre, and 53% provided dance instruction at least once weekly (Parsad, Spiegelman, & Coopersmith, 2012). Too often arts education has been reduced due to budget cuts, reallocation of resources, and an increased emphasis on core content, such as language arts and math (Hourigan, 2014). In schools where poverty is not necessarily a factor, the emphasis on standardized testing and meeting state and federal benchmarks has prompted the reallocation of instructional time; "testing—and practice for test-taking—consumes an inordinate amount of time, taking the place of arts and athletic programs" (Schneider & Curl, 2013, para 5). Educators and education researchers recognize that a weekly 45-minute art or music class "is not enough to impact [students] socially, emotionally, or cognitively" (Trafí-Prats & Woywod, 2013, p. 11). This is especially problematic for elementary schools in locations, such as Illinois, Washington, D.C., and California, which have limited art instructional time, even if they do meet weekly (Chappell & Cahnmann-Taylor, 2013; Rabkin & Hedberg, 2011). As Chappell and Cahnmann-Taylor (2013) contended:

> limited access to arts in schools tends to have the greatest impact on minoritized youth, who tend to be hypersegregated in schools with more limited budgets, less culturally and linguistically responsive practices, and highly controlled curriculum based on discrete skill development.
>
> (p. 245)

Even when underprivileged youth have an option to select their schools, there are negative consequences when it comes to arts education writ large. With the voucher system in place (and potentially expanding even more with the new White House administration), low-income families may become empowered to select schools beyond their neighborhood, but, in so doing, they are "tak[ing] their resources to another school, [and] stripping the community-based schools of funds" (Hourigan, 2014, p. 36). In essence, for the youth who attend other schools, it is unclear what arts instruction they may receive, and the already marginalized youth left behind will experience increased marginalization because there will be fewer programs available, namely arts and special education opportunities: "At the very least, students will be taking funds that are used to support programs in areas such as the arts or special education and, at least in part, moving them into schools (sometimes religious schools) that are not mandated to provide either program" (Hourigan, 2014, p. 36).

Why Arts Education?

In his speech, "Why the Arts Must Be at the Table," Rip Rapson (2016), president of the private philanthropic Kresge Foundation, provided three overarching reasons why the arts are a necessity in contemporary society and the "new reality." First, the arts help to support social and cultural appreciation because of "their power to avow and fortify bedrock values of community tolerance, cohesion, and inclusion" (para 12). This harkens back to the humanizing and democratizing aspects of the arts and arts instruction (Chappell & Cahnmann-Taylor, 2013). Relatedly, Rapson acknowledged that the creativity inherent in the arts "propel[s] us inexorably toward constructively disruptive civic reflection . . . to wrestle with what is good and what is bad, what is false and what true" (para 20, 22). Through innovative and creative work, students can interrogate and reconceptualize reality and feel a sense of "creative placemaking" (para 25). Connecting to community, a place, or shared experience creates a "magnetic pull" and commitment, and this type of connection is equally important to raising social consciousness. Furthermore, Rapson emphasized how the arts can nurture forward thinking and leadership that are necessary to support the future and well-being of the community; he contended, "cultural creativity may well become the driving force of community revitalization. It promises more adaptive ways of seeing, understanding, experiencing, and transforming where we live . . . how we work . . . what we dream" (para 31, ellipses in original). In essence, Rapson's speech underscored that arts education promotes a future citizenry of leaders who critically evaluate marginalizing structures, value democratized approaches, and honor the local while considering the global. At the heart of Rapson's discussion is the importance of celebrating and sustaining creativity, experimentation, and tolerance.

In this and other ways, the inclusion of the arts has been linked to social and emotional learning (Brouillette, 2010). As Cratsley (2017) acknowledged, "When implemented well, the arts bring a sense of community into the classroom, foster decision-making skills, and promote cultural awareness that transcends the walls of the school" (para 8). An awareness of self and others is part of social-emotional learning (SEL), which highlights the need for students to "become culturally literate, intellectually reflective, and lifelong learners" (Weissberg, Durlak, Domitrovich, & Gullotta, 2015, pp. 4–5). Arts education helps to refine what the Collaborative for Academic, Social, and Emotional Learning (CASEL) indicates as the five "competencies" of SEL: "self-awareness, self-management, social awareness, relationship skills, and responsible decision making" (Weissberg & Cascarino, 2013, p. 10). More specifically, when partaking in arts education, students engage in iterative learning that involves self-assessment, reflection, persistence, and innovative and expansive thinking (Winner & Hetland, 2009). Furthermore, the visual arts help students to evaluate preconceptions and keep an open mind by "breaking away from stereotypes and seeing accurately and directly" (Winner & Hetland, 2009, p. 3). Such skills are essential for helping students evaluate the world around them and consider creative and alternative solutions and resolutions to local and global issues. In other words, the arts are key to students' social, emotional, and education futures.

Makerspaces and Arts Education

When considering the arts with regard to education futures, one may turn to the maker movement, a campaign to engage students in building, making, and exploring in general and, more recently, developing capacities within the STEM (science, technology, engineering, and mathematics) fields. Creativity, expression, and experimentation are all part of arts education, but they are also inherent activities within a makerspace, or a "physical location where people gather to share resources and knowledge, work on projects, network, and build" (Educause Learning Initiative, 2013). Halverson and Sheridan (2014) define the maker movement as "the growing number of people who are engaged in the creative production of artifacts in their daily lives and who find physical and digital forums to share their processes and products with others" (p. 496). Within makerspaces, there is emphasis on creating and "tinkering" (Daley & Child, 2015), and, even at an early age, when children participate in "making," they engage in critical thinking, collaborative problem solving, and social awareness:

> Children tinker as they take things apart, put things together, figure out how things work, and attempt to build and make creations using tools. When they are faced with a problem, children ask questions, make plans, work together, test their ideas, solve problems, improve their ideas to make them better, and share their ideas and creations with others. These are the thinking processes and actions that scientists and engineers use to solve real-world problems with real-world constraints, including limited materials, time, and funds.
>
> (Heroman, 2017, p. 72)

Elementary education could and should include such approaches without necessarily naming them makerspace-related practices—after all, the Deweyan (1938/1997) concept of learning-by-doing has been part of constructivist (Vygotsky, 1978) and constructionist (Papert, 1980)[1] approaches well before "makerspaces" entered the scene. However, the movement to include makerspaces has called attention to practical skills and thoughtful deliberations essential in and beyond the classroom.

Though the concepts of making and tinkering are well-known aspects of learning-by-doing, the specific maker movement has been traced to the 2005 debut of the magazine, *Make:* (Burke, 2015). The *Make:* website claims its stake in the maker movement as well, noting, "Make: is the magazine for Makers, which was first published in 2005 and used the word 'Maker' to name the community" (How it all began, 2017). It wasn't until at least one decade into the 21st century that education and library-related research began to focus more readily on learning in the makerspace. Now, the makerspace has a buzzword connotation that portends increased engagement, focused yet fluid building, and private and public funding for arts-related production. Yet the terms "arts education" and "makerspaces" do not seem to be used synonymously. Perhaps this is because the maker movement has generated attention to STEM-related making, as "makerspaces tend to be oriented towards the use of digital technologies, although most also incorporate more traditional ways of making, incorporating electronic circuit-building and wood-working, for example" (Sweeny, 2017, p. 3). Or maybe it is because makerspaces can be anywhere—not necessarily in a school—and can engage learners of all ages in collaboration and (re)invention; the materials and art-related components seem secondary to the ethos of the maker movement. The irony is, however, that the ethos of arts education and its social and emotional implications have direct and indirect connections to the ethos of the maker movement.

Sweeny (2017) suggested that the recognition of specific artists, along with reconceptualizing traditional art resources in light of digital ones, are steps needed to bridge traditional arts education and the maker movement. Likewise, Wohlwend, Keune, and Peppler (2016) contended that they "see the Maker Movement as an opportunity to infuse technology into early childhood curricula through teachers' expertise in familiar staples of early childhood education: dramatic play and exploratory design with art materials" (p. 85). Though possibilities abound, digital technologies are not requisite components of all makerspaces, and, even without the digital component, there are still inherent areas of overlap when it comes to process learning, imagination, and creativity in arts education and makerspace practices. Regardless of the reason the two have been addressed separately, calls to explore the ways arts education and the maker movement work "synergistically" (Clapp & Jimenez, 2013) suggest that the future of arts education may (or perhaps should) include makerspace language and vice versa.

A more expansive view of the maker movement reveals an overall emphasis on hands-on learning and opportunities for individual and collaborative building experiences. Makerspaces "provide a place for students to explore questions, bounce ideas off one another, build something together and fail and try again, all in a safe, creative environment" (Smay & Walker, 2015). Learners reflect on their practice, engage in iterative learning, and manage personal growth and collective partnerships. At the core of the makerspace ethos, then, is the combination of collaboration and interest-driven "process- and product-oriented practices" in spaces with a range of formal-to-informal instructional structures (Sheridan et al., 2014, p. 527). The emphasis on the process of learning and sharing is critical, and the maker movement has a democratizing aspect (Hatch, 2014). What's more, as Sheffield, Koul, Blackley, and Maynard (2017) underscored, makerspaces may potentially flatten hierarchies, as there "is no expert voice due to the organic nature of Makerspaces" and the makerspace has "the potential to empower young people to become agents of change in their communities" (p. 150).

In a similar vein, the maker movement values the voice, the ideas, and the action of those who create, ideate, and re-create:

> Our own experience as a creator, a maker, a producer can change the world in small but significant ways, and we may not realize it at the time. It can also profoundly change how we think about ourselves, and that kind of change may be the most profound. We develop a sense that our ideas matter, that they can impact us and the world around us.
>
> (Dougherty & Conrad, 2016, p. 143)

The problem solving that Dougherty and Conrad addressed, namely looking beyond the self to consider local and global issues, echoes many of the sentiments Winner and Hetland (2009) noted about arts education. Changing mindsets and developing social responsibility are important parts of social and emotional learning, as well as the growth of a generation interested in being agents of change.

Relatedly, Dougherty (2013) underscored how a maker mindset honors iterative and process learning and the important tensions that exist when success and growth hinge on challenge, experimentation, failure, and reflection. The maker mindset

> is the process of iterating over a project to improve it. It is a chance to participate in communities of makers of all ages by sharing your work and expertise. Making can be a compelling social experience, built around relationships.
>
> (2013, p. 9)

In other words, the maker movement is not simply about haphazard tinkering with blocks, connecting circuits, or cutting paper into different shapes. There are implicit and explicit goals supported by the space, time, and fortitude to take risks and explore outcomes. Whereas arts education may promote the same type of experimentation and flexible foci, the connection between arts education and makerspace practices needs further investigation.

Additionally, instruction and/or assistance in makerspaces needs greater examination. In their two-year ethnography of a "Making 4 Change" program to benefit the greater community, Barton, Tan, and Greenberg (2017) found that the students needed such attention and oversight that the researchers were "convinced that an intense level of adult attention is necessary in order to productively engage with individual youth in ways that honor how they bring their particular interests and experiences to bear on the making enterprise" (p. 15). Likewise, in their examination of three makerspaces, Sheridan and colleagues (2014) addressed the need for scaffolding and guided assistance. For example, the authors noted that during a sewing and embroidery Makeshop session, one child could not determine what he should make, and he needed modeling and guidance to identify an objective: "After practicing, he wanted to make something, but didn't know what . . . The facilitator brought over a ball he had sewn, and the child decided he wanted to make a similar one" (p. 520). Even when formal instruction was not an overt component, Sheridan and colleagues found that facilitators mentored by tinkering in front of youth, thereby creating informal learning experiences for youth to observe and ask related questions. Moreover, the researchers noted that, despite the initial arrangement of the Makershop, collaboration and flexibility became an important component to meet the needs of the learners:

> One of the distinctive features of all these spaces is the way diverse learning arrangements (e.g., solo exploration, facilitated one-on-one or small group projects, collaborative projects, online forums, and structure classes) often informally evolve to support the projects and goals of the participants.
>
> (p. 521)

What comes to the fore, in other words, is that meaning making does not simply happen in a makerspace. Participation in interest-driven activities, supported by various forms of mentorship, facilitation, and/or guidance, often leads to meaningful learning.

Fleming (2015) explained that, in addition to planning makerspace activities, teachers should plan to be part of students' collaborative work, promoting student engagement and student-driven learning. Though Fleming's suggestions have merit, some seem to be too structured. There needs to be flexible time and space for experimentation and tangential work that may lead to new discoveries. After all, the success of the makerspace is also dependent upon students' ability to take risks and tinker; as Barton, Tan, and Greenberg (2017) contended, with "mutual, sustained forms of engagement [with others], youth will have access to a more expansive space to learn and become in making" (p. 19).

Despite promises of agency, change, leadership, and democratizing practices, there is troubling discourse around makerspaces that suggest that "making" is "a uniquely American activity focused on technological forms of innovation that advance hands-on learning and contribute to the growth of the economy" (Vossoughi, Hooper, & Escudé, 2016, p. 207) that belies the work tradespeople engage in via hands-on professions and the trades and skills often acquired outside the United States. In other words, there are many who could bring to the makerspace their knowledge of making and tinkering. However, the way makerspaces are featured and the practices they honor may exclude and disempower marginalized populations:

> The modes of inclusion practiced by the maker movement . . . which often reach out to and invite in participants who may have a very different historical and economic relationship to making and working with

one's hands. In the process, working-class communities of color are once again positioned as targets of intervention rather than sources of deep knowledge and skill, and dominant communities are reinscribed as being ahead, with something to teach or offer rather than something to learn.

(Vossoughi, Hooper, & Escudé, 2016, p. 212)

Though the maker movement may include opportunities to flatten hierarchies and empower learners, until all acts of making and until the discourses used honor all learners and diverse cultures, the approach may not be as democratizing as intended. Furthermore, when the maker movement focuses on expensive tools typically associated with STEM subjects (e.g., 3D printers and electronic invention kits), the programs do not honor "ingenuity present in communities that are not benefiting from dominant economic structures—such as material repair and trade, hacking, making as social or artistic practice, and economic survival" (Vossoughi, Hooper, & Escudé, 2016, p. 208). Though some boast the creation of makerspaces can be completed with a $500 budget (Fontichiaro, 2016), the design and implementation of new schools that include blended approaches and spaces for collaboration and making may feature architecture and furnishings that can be a large and expensive undertaking as designers contemplate the integration of irregular-shaped classrooms, sound-proof rooms, and glass walls that enable students to be inspired by the outdoors (Kearns, 2017).

The five competencies of social and emotional learning—self-awareness, self-management, social awareness, relationship skills, and responsible decision making—may provide educators, education researchers, designers, and policy makers alike with the language and focus to help illuminate issues of (in)equity, challenge discourses that privilege dominant cultures, generate openness to diversity, and support the development of personal and social responsibility.

Where Do We Go From Here?

In addition to considering the maker movement in light of social and emotional learning, educators and designers may look more closely at the overlap between arts education and the maker movement. Doing so might highlight the inequities that exist, as "play- and discovery-oriented activities found in makerspaces are limited in formal education settings, particularly in poorer schools" (Oliver, 2016, p. 164); however, focusing on both arts education and makerspaces as a combined approach may help to draw the necessary attention to the current inequities. Yet, attention needs to be prudent, precise, and pointed; otherwise, miscommunication and misdirection may obscure the possible short- and long-term benefits for education futures.

For example, the Obama administration highlighted the arts, as well as the maker movement. In 2014, the White House hosted the first Maker

Faire and President Obama "declared June 18 the National Day of Making" (Make: Day of Making). In that same year, the White House hosted a Turnaround Arts program talent show, which required a transformation of space: "The East Room, typically a showcase for a portrait of Martha Washington, was bathed in neon orange, green and red lights and served as a stage on Tuesday afternoon. A piano player sat in the corner" (Thompson, 2014, para 2). Though both efforts are commendable, the arts and making are treated as an anomaly, not the norm. If the arts and making are part of everyday meaning making, then designating a day to celebrate the activities may raise temporary (and perhaps artificial) consciousness but potentially make discovery-based learning seem like the exception and not the rule.

Related coverage of the Turnaround Arts program also seemed to draw upon the extremes; Thompson's article provided a description of a traditional room temporarily transformed by the gleam of bright neon lights. Another *Washington Post* article began a depiction of two children "wandering around on stilts, costumed as masked scarecrow-like monsters, like unexplained extras in a European art film, their presence somehow part of the whole artistic process" (Midgette, 2013, para 2). The language Midgette used suggests a haphazard approach to art that is both unconvincing and perhaps ineffective (e.g., "unexplained extras" and "somehow part of the whole artistic process"). A more recent article about a Turnaround Arts program (Larimer, 2017) specifically juxtaposed "little touches," like displays of children's artwork, with the unsubtle noise that permeated the halls: "And there is this: It often is not super quiet around here" (para 2). What these examples suggest is that arts education is not necessarily considered a standard practice, yet arts education and the maker movement need not be radical or controversial. Stilts can still be part of the conversation, but the arts need less sensationalizing and more permanence. Otherwise, arts education and makerspace activities will be more of a trend and less of a movement, and both need to be mainstays in education, particularly if creativity, collaboration, and innovation are to be accepted forms of practice in schools, especially those that serve underrepresented children.

Furthermore, the connection between the arts and makerspace activities needs greater examination, with additional focus on integration. Though the concept of STEAM (instead of STEM) helps to insert the arts into the equation, there is a need for greater integration of arts across the disciplines without an assessment culture extinguishing the innovation in the discovery-based practices. Honey and Kanter (2013) explained that this is possible through interdisciplinary learning that engages students as investigators:

> Early in school, however, this spark—what psychologists have dubbed intrinsic motivation—is all-too-frequently extinguished by the extrinsic goals and expectations of school. Fortunately there is research-based evidence that says it is possible to rekindle this natural motivation to learn by designing environments that are supportive, that engage learners in

meaningful activities, that lessen a student's anxiety and fear, and that provide a level of challenge matched to student's skills . . . we must move away from the current system of "telling" students about science to helping students gain critical problem solving and inquiry skills in the contexts of relevant, real-world, interdisciplinary problems.

(pp. 2–3)

Overall, arts education that involves discovery-based learning and tinkering, therefore, may require a paradigm shift that dispels the dispassionate standardization of assessment culture and supports flexible and reflective thinking, collaborative problem solving, and social responsibility, as these and related mindsets and practices are inherent necessities in students' education futures. Finally, though resources are an important component to consider, if the emphasis on tinkering and expression—not the resources per se—is at the heart of exploration, then the ethos of the arts and of the maker movement may, in fact, help to democratize education and bridge existing inequity gaps.

Note

1 Though the debate between constructivist and constructionist principles extends beyond the scope of this chapter, it is important to note that the maker movement is supported by and rooted in theories of making and learning that account for interacting with the world and using tools to construct knowledge.

References

About us. (n.d.). Turnaround Arts: Creating success in schools. Retrieved from http://turnaroundarts.kennedy-center.org.

Barton, A. C., Tan, E., & Greenberg, D. (2017). The makerspace movement: Sites of possibilities for equitable opportunities to engage underrepresented youth in STEM. *Teachers College Record, 119*(6), 1–44.

Bowen, D. H., Greene, J. P., & Kisida, B. (2014). Learning to think critically: A visual art experiment. *Educational Researcher, 43*(1), 37–44. doi.org/10.3102/00 13189X13512675.

Brouillette, L. (2010). How the arts help children to create healthy social scripts: Exploring the perceptions of elementary teachers. *Arts Education Policy Review, 111*(1), 16–24.

Brown, E. D., & Sax, K. L. (2013). Arts enrichment and preschool emotions for low-income children at risk. *Early Childhood Research Quarterly, 28*(2), 337–346. doi.org/10.1016/j.ecresq. 2012.08.002.

Burke, J. (2015). *Making sense: Can makerspaces work in academic libraries?* Paper presented at Association for College & Research Libraries (ACRL). Retrieved from www.ala.org/acrl/acrl/conferences/acrl2015/papers.

Catterall, J. S. (2009). Doing well and doing good by doing art: The effects of education in the visual and performing arts on the achievements and values of young adults. Los Angeles, CA/London: Imagination Group/I-Group Books.

Chappell, S. V., & Cahnmann-Taylor, M. (2013). No child left with crayons: The imperative of arts-based education and research with language "minority" and other minoritized communities. *Review of Research in Education, 37,* 243–268.

Clapp, E. P., & Jimenez, R. L. (2013). Letters to the editor. *Art Education, 66*(6), 5.

Cratsley, L. (2017). Access to arts education: An overlooked tool for social-emotional learning and positive school climate. *Alliance for Excellent Education.* Retrieved from https://all4ed.org/access-to-arts-education-an-overlooked-tool-for-social-emotional-learning-and-positive-school-climate.

Daley, M., & Child, J. (2015). Makerspaces in the school library environment. *Access, 29*(1), 42–49.

Davis, J. H. (2008). *Why our schools need the arts.* New York: Teachers College Press.

Dewey, J. (1938/1997). *Experience & education.* New York: Touchstone.

Dougherty, D. (2013). The maker mindset. In M. Honey & D. E. Kanter (Eds.), *Design, make, play: Growing the next generation of STEM innovators* (pp. 7–11). New York: Routledge.

Dougherty, D., & Conrad, A. (2016). Free to make: How the maker movement is changing our schools, our jobs, and our minds. Berkeley, CA: North Atlantic Books.

Educause Learning Initiative. (2013). 7 things you should know about makerspaces. *Educause.* Retrieved from https://library.educause.edu/resources/2013/4/7-things-you-should-know-about-makerspaces.

Fleming, L. (2015). Worlds of making: Best practices for establishing a makerspace for your school. Thousand Oaks, CA: Corwin.

Fontichiaro, K. (2016). Help! My principal says I need to start a makerspace in my elementary library! *Teacher Librarian, 44*(1), 49–51.

Glass, D., Meyer, A., & Rose, D. H. (2013). Universal design for learning and the arts. *Harvard Educational Review, 83*(1), 98–119. doi.org/10.17763/haer.83.1.33102p26478p54pw.

Halverson, E. R., & Sheridan, K. M. (2014). The maker movement in education. *Harvard Educational Review, 84*(4), 495–504. doi.org/10.17763/haer.84.4.34j1g68140382063.

Hatch, M. (2014). The maker movement manifesto: Rules for innovation in the new world of crafters, hackers, and tinkerers. New York: McGraw-Hill.

Heroman, C. (2017). Making and tinkering: Bringing design challenges to the classroom. *Young Children, 72*(2), 72–75, 78–79.

Hetland, L., Winner, E., Veenema, S., & Sheridan, K. M. (2013). *Studio thinking 2: The real benefits of visual arts education* (2nd ed.). New York: Teachers College Press.

Honey, M., & Kanter, D. E. (2013). Design, make, play: Growing the next generation of science innovators. In M. Honey & D. E. Kanter (Eds.), *Design, make, play: Growing the next generation of STEM innovators* (pp. 1–6). New York: Routledge.

Hourigan, R. M. (2014). Intersections between school reform, the arts, and special education: The children left behind. *Arts Education Policy Review, 115*(2), 35–38. doi.org/10.1080/10632913.2014.883892.

How it all began. (2017). *Make: We are all makers.* Retrieved from https://makermedia.com/?utm_source=makezine&utm_campaign=makezinefooter.

Impact. (n.d.). Turnaround Arts: Creating success in schools. Retrieved from http://turnaroundarts.kennedy-center.org/impact.

Kearns, L. (2017). New blueprints for K-12 schools. *Education Next, 17*(3). Retrieved from http://educationnext.org/new-blueprints-k-12-schools-innovative-design-supports-blended-learning.

Kraehe, A. M., Acuff, J. B., & Travis, S. (2016). Equity, the arts, and urban education: A review. *Urban Review, 48*(2), 220–244. doi.org/10.1007/s11256-016-0352-2.

Larimer, S. (2017). How a former White House photographer helped these D.C. kids learn. *The Washington Post*. Retrieved from www.washingtonpost.com/local/education/how-a-former-white-house-photographer-helped-these-dc-kids-learn/2017/12/10/22660dee-dc2e-11e7-b859-fb0995360725_story.html?utm_term=.52b7f3c60e7e.

Make: Day of Making. (n.d.). *Make:* Retrieved from https://makezine.com/day-of-making.

Midgette, A. (2013). WP Magazine, the education issue: After years of crouching, arts ed is raising its hand again. *The Washington Post*. Retrieved from www.washingtonpost.com/blogs/liveblog/wp/2013/02/21/magazine-the-education-issue-after-years-of-crouching-arts-ed-is-raising-its-hand-again/?utm_term=.4c9ff6f5a514.

Oliver, K. M. (2016). Professional development considerations for makerspace leaders, part one: Addressing "what?" and "why?" *TechTrends, 60*(2), 160–166. doi.org/10.1007/s11528-016-0028-5.

Papert, S. (1980). Mindstorms: Children, computers, and powerful Ideas. New York: Basic Books.

Parsad, B., Spiegelman, M., & Coopersmith, J. (2012). Arts Education in Public Elementary and Secondary Schools 1999–2000 and 2009–10. *National Center for Education Statistics*. Retrieved from https://nces.ed.gov/pubs2012/2012014rev.pdf.

Rabkin, N., & Hedberg, E. C. (2011). Arts education in America: What the declines mean for arts participation. Research Report #52. Washington, D.C.: National Endowment for the Arts. Retrieved from www.venicearts.org/assets/media/27037.pdf.

Rapson, R. (2016). Why the arts must be at the table. *President's Committee on the Arts and the Humanities*. Retrieved from https://nces.ed.gov/pubs2012/2012014rev.pdf.

Schneider, J., & Curl, H. (2013). What poor children need in school. *The Washington Post*. Retrieved from www.washingtonpost.com/news/answer-sheet/wp/2013/10/18/what-poor-children-need-in-school/?utm_term=.5528a989e149.

Sheffield, R., Koul, R., Blackley, S., & Maynard, N. (2017). Makerspace in STEM for girls: A physical space to develop twenty-first century skills. *Educational Media International, 54*(2), 148–164. doi.org/10.1080/09523987.2017.1362812.

Sheridan, K. M., Halverson, E. R., Litts, B. K., Brahms, L., Jacobs-Priebe, L., & Owens, T. (2014). Learning in the making: A comparative case study of three makerspaces. *Harvard Educational Review, 84*(4), 505–531. doi.org/10.17763/haer.84.4.brr34733723j648u.

Smay, D., & Walker, C. (2015). Makerspaces as a creative approach to education. *Teacher Librarian, 42*(4), 39–43.

Sweeny, R. W. (2017). Making and breaking in an art education makerspace. *Journal of Innovation and Entrepreneurship, 6*(9), 1–10. doi.org/10.1186/s13731-017-0071-2.

Thompson, K. (2014). Students in "Turnaround Arts" program hold a talent show in the White House. *The Washington Post*. Retrieved from www.washingtonpost.

com/lifestyle/style/students-in-turnaround-arts-program-hold-a-talent-show-in-the-white-house/2014/05/20/01dd3a7e-e061-11e3-810f-764fe508b82d_story.html?utm_term=.6f2b5f5a4a73.

Trafi-Prats, L., & Woywod, C. (2013). We love our public schools: Art teachers' life histories in a time of loss, accountability, and new commonalities. *Studies in Art Education*, *55*(1), 7–17.

Vossoughi, S., Hooper, P. K., & Escudé, M. (2016). Making through the lens of culture and power: Toward transformative visions of educational equity. *Harvard Educational Review*, *86*(2). doi.org/10.17763/0017-8055.86.2.206.

Vygotsky, L. S. (1978). Mind in society: The development of higher psychological processes. Cambridge, MA: Harvard University Press.

Weissberg, R. P., & Cascarino, J. (2013). Academic learning + social-emotional learning = national priority. *Kappan*, *95*(2), 8–13.

Weissberg, R. P., Durlak, J. A., Domitrovich, C. E., & Gullotta, T. P. (2015). Social and emotional learning: Past, present and future. In J. A. Durlak, C. E. Domitrovich, R. P. Weissberg, & T. P. Gullotta (Eds.), *Handbook of social and emotional learning: Research and practice* (pp. 3–19). New York: The Guilford Press.

Wexler, A. (2014). Reaching higher? The impact of Common Core State Standards on the visual arts, poverty, and disabilities. *Arts Education Policy Review*, *115*(2), 52–61. doi.org/10.1080/10632913.2014.883897.

Winner, E., & Hetland, L. (2009). Art for our sake: School art classes matter more than ever – but not for the reasons you think. *Colleagues*, *4*(2), 1–4. Retrieved from https://scholarworks.gvsu.edu/colleagues/vol4/iss2/5.

Wohlwend, K. E., Keune, A., & Peppler, K. (2016). Design playshop: Preschoolers making, playing and learning with squishy circuits. In K. Peppler, E. R. Halverson, & Y. B. Kafai (Eds.), *Makeology: Makerspaces as learning environments* (pp. 83–96). New York: Routledge.

9 Sports and Recreation

Inequalities for Young Children with Regards to Sports and Physical Activity

Elizabeth Chase

Introduction

In the middle of President Obama's first term in the White House, the First Lady, Michelle Obama, launched a laudable campaign to address childhood obesity. The *Let's Move!* program put the First Lady's star power in a leading role for the national public awareness effort to improve the health of the nation's children. The campaign brought a pressing issue to the fore: childhood obesity, physical activity, and access to healthful, nutritious food. These issues were as timely in 2010, when the *Let's Move!* campaign began, as they are right now. Childhood obesity rates, though declining slightly in recent years (Cheung, Cunningham, Narayan, & Kramer, 2016), have tripled since 1970, with a current incidence of obesity at 20% for school-aged children (Ogden et al., 2016). The benefits of physical activity for children and adults alike have been well touted in the mainstream media as well as in academic research (Janssen & LeBlanc, 2010). Physical activity for young children is associated with academic benefits throughout their years in school (Carlson et al., 2008) and has been identified as a key factor in maintaining a healthy weight and engaging in positive social interactions (Allendar, Cowburn, & Foster, 2006).

Given the positive evidence for physical activity, movement, and access to recreational sports, this chapter explores the issues surrounding physical activity in the early years. Specifically, this chapter addresses issues of access and equality with regard to young children, sports, and recreational/physical activity. In so doing, the chapter puts forth exploratory answers to the following three questions:

1) What does the extant research say about expectations for and access to physical activity in the early years?
2) Given a certain set of inequalities in access and experience for different groups of children, what are the effects of these inequalities?
3) What solutions can be suggested for reducing these inequalities?

Expectations for Physical Activity

The Society of Health and Physical Educators (SHAPE) offers a set of national standards for K–12 physical education and provides a set of guidelines for children from birth through age 5. These guidelines indicate a variety of outcomes for different age groups of children. Among the notable recommendations, SHAPE suggests that:

- Infants interact with caregivers in physical activities that are dedicated to exploring movement and the environment, and that these activities promote skill development in movement
- Toddlers engage in 30 minutes of daily structured physical activity (both indoor and outdoor) and 60 minutes of daily unstructured physical activity with peers and caregivers
- Preschoolers engage in 60 minutes of structured physical activity and 60 minutes of unstructured physical activity each day, and that their physical activities allow for development of motor skills.

(More information can be found at www.shapeamerica.org)

These guidelines represent a minimum standard of activity and movement for children from birth to age 5, and they provide a snapshot of the expectations for the amount of time that young children should be engaged in physical activity.

For children under the age of 5, nearly all of their physical activity takes place under adult supervision, either at home or in a daycare, nursery, or pre-kindergarten setting. Schools, and by extension daycare and nursery settings, are typically identified as institutions holding a primary responsibility for encouraging and providing opportunities for physical activity for young children (McKenzie & Kahan, 2008). These opportunities range from structured engagements such as a physical education class or sports club, to leisurely activities before or after school, or at recess. Young children are given frequent opportunities to engage in play—either active or more sedentary—while they are in structured school settings. For students in elementary school, the focus on testing and accountability has driven a culture in which seated deskwork has infringed on the time and space normally given to physical education and activity. For programs as early as pre-kindergarten, financial and structural changes can be felt in the face of an overwhelming focus on academic needs and what is often described as a "core" curriculum (McKenzie & Kahan, 2008).

Given the expectations for physical activity outlined above, it is important to address certain limitations in this exploration of young children's experience with sports, recreation, and physical activity. First, programs for young children are abundant in our country at this time (Stork & Sanders, 2008). While all programs must be certified and registered with a state licensing board, there is no national standard to which programs must adhere, and therefore there is great divergence of experience among programs. This presents an enormous challenge to parents in choosing a program for their young children, and it also presents a problem of generalizability within this chapter. Without the ability to survey a wide swath of school-based and community-based programs in order to aggregate the results, this chapter is thus restricted to snapshots of physical activities and opportunities for young children. Second, the kinds of experiences that young children have with physical activity and physical education vary widely and are influenced by many factors. These factors include, but are not limited to, race, class, dis/ability, parental/caregiver involvement, socio-economic status, access to affordable housing, access to school-based or community-based programs, and parental employment. It is similarly outside of the scope of this chapter to address the sum of these factors in depth or to address even a small portion of them in part. Instead, this chapter provides a series of snapshots of some of the issues concerning equitable access to physical activity and physical education for young children today.

Access to Physical Activity and Education

This section examines the kinds of programs that are commonly available to young children and their families and explores the levels of access that children have. Researchers have noted that access to physical activity and education for children is unevenly distributed (Stork & Sanders, 2008). Further, training and supervision for instructors and leaders within community and school-based programs vary greatly. The instructors and childcare providers in school-based and community-based centers for young children are rarely trained in early childhood physical education. Most often, these instructors are providing care in the form of keeping the children safe and supervised rather than engaging in teaching strategies that attend to the physical and developmental needs of young children (Stork & Sanders, 2008). Additionally, the programs may not be designed to address the needs of children with varying physical and developmental abilities, which limits their accessibility and ease of use for many families.

Recess

Researchers have noted that the quality and amount of free play for young children have changed over the past few generations (Burdette & Whitaker, 2005). Likely influenced by changing social habits and increased access to electronic devices, the amount of time that young children spend roaming the outdoors and inventing their own forms of play has declined in many communities close to or in major metropolitan areas. For very young children, researchers advocate a return of play that is unstructured but supervised.

This kind of play is often found in the school day under the heading of recess. Recess, which some consider the fourth R (in addition to reading, 'riting, and 'rithmetic), provides opportunities for physical activity, social interaction, cooperation, and creative problem solving (McKenzie & Kahan, 2008). And yet, access to recess and experience while in recess is also unevenly distributed. Children from disadvantaged backgrounds are more likely to attend schools with facilities that are old and broken-down, and with equipment that is shabby and minimal (Fernandes & Sturm, 2010). The lack of consistency and quality in equipment and facilities means that less time is spent in recess, providing significant barriers to physical activity and education. To understand the serious consequences of a lack of resources on the quality of school facilities and equipment, readers can explore Kozol's (1991) *Savage Inequalities: Children in America's Schools* and Johnson and Johnson's (2006) *High Stakes: Poverty, Testing, and Failure in American Schools*. Each of these texts shines a bright light on the unforgiving outcomes of unequal resource distribution in our nation's schools. Most notably for the purposes of this chapter, these two texts illustrate how children in under-resourced schools have far less access to the facilities and equipment that promote engaging, pleasurable, and beneficial physical activities and education.

In addition to the issue of facilities and equipment, time for recess is often compromised for academic work that is considered to be more important, particularly with regards to performance on state-administered standardized tests. In many schools, teachers and administrators are struggling to figure out appropriate responses to standardized tests. Given the high stakes that are associated with these tests (e.g., ratings for teachers and schools, more (or less) pay depending on student performance), it is no wonder that teachers, administrators, and other district-level personnel have explicitly and implicitly responded to these pressures with curriculum narrowing (Berliner, 2011). Curriculum narrowing, in its most basic form, is a way of restricting the curriculum to address topics and items that will be assessed on standardized tests. In older grades, this has the deleterious effect of increasing time on "core" academic subjects to the detriment of art, music, technology, drama, sports, physical education, and the list goes on. In the younger grades, the effects of curriculum narrowing can be felt in more time spent on topics and subjects that are considered academic and less time spent on play, creativity, mess-making, and centers (Jarrett, 2002).

Ohanian (2002) provides a practitioner perspective on the obsessive mania with testing, exploring the unfortunate consequences in many schools, such as the reduction of play and recess in favor of more time "on task" with academic subjects. This text, among others that address recess for young children, illustrates the importance of play, creativity, and social interaction for all children, but particularly young ones. Given the intense focus on standardized testing and accountability measures that accompany it, recess provides a needed break from the rigors of the school day and also provides an important respite from the number of minutes children spend on seated, desk work. Schools such as the ones depicted in *Savage Inequalities* and *High Stakes* are under-funded and under-resourced at baseline. This means that equipment and facilities are in short supply. Further, performance on standardized tests in these schools is typically lower than performance levels at highly funded, well-resourced public and private schools. These factors combine to create situations in which children attending under-resourced schools are put at double jeopardy for the loss of recess and unstructured play: first because the facilities and equipment are sub-standard to begin with, and second because an intense focus on test scores and performance increases the likelihood of curriculum narrowing at the expense of recess and physical activity. Researchers continue to sound the alarm on the elimination of unstructured play, and they also warn that a child's access to this time should never be taken away for punitive or academic reasons (Ramstetter, Murray, & Garner, 2010).

Screen Time

Screen time is an important factor to consider in evaluating the opportunities for physical activity and physical education among young children. In a study that analyzed time spent on screens and time spent engaged in physical activity for over 1,000 preschoolers in Australia, Hinkley, Salmon, Okely, Crawford, and Hesketh (2012) found that less than one-third of participants met general guidelines for time spent in physical activity. The majority of children, therefore, are spending too much time with screen-based entertainment and inadequate time with physical activity, an imbalance that is likely to be exacerbated with time as children get older and increase their screen habits. The authors note that strategies are needed to promote physical activity and reduce screen-based entertainment in young children (Hinkley et al., 2012). Similarly, in a study of young children's activity time and screen time, researchers in the United States found that a majority of children had physical activity and screen time behaviors that were lopsided, meaning more time was spent on screens and less time on activity in relation to the recommendations. Further, these researchers found that these behaviors were worse for children in three sub-groups: female, Black, or already overweight (Anderson, Economos, & Must, 2008).

Parents and caregivers play a primary role in monitoring and reducing screen time for young children. There is limited research on screen time and young children, and most researchers agree on calling for further inquiry in this area. It is important to note that future research would benefit from avoiding deficit assumptions about parenting, which can suggest that the way to increase physical activity and reduce screen time is through improving parenting practices and changing parenting styles (see Xu, Wen, & Rissel, 2015). Rather than focus on what parents lack in their approach to reducing screen time, a more critical and robust examination would and should focus on the socio-demographic factors that are important targets for promoting healthy and active lifestyles among children and their families (see Carson, Rosu, & Janssen, 2014).

Financial Impacts and Costs

In 2014, the United States Census Bureau reported that the median household income was just under $52,000 per year. The federal government sets the poverty line each year, marking the number at which a family is eligible for government programs and benefits that include financial savings and supports. In 2017, a two-person household met the federal poverty line at just under $19,000 of annual income. And a whopping 45 million people, or 14% of all Americans, lived below the poverty line as reported in the 2014 Census. At or below the poverty line, there is no room for luxuries as even basic necessities become costs for which supports and savings are needed. Federal programs provide support for food, health care, and housing, but these supports are accompanied by a certain amount of bureaucratic hassle and restriction. They are subject to change frequently and they do not cover what would ordinarily be thought of as extras, including access to sports and physical education.

A sampling of costs for sports classes can help illustrate the challenge of providing such activities to children for the majority of families who are below the median household income or closer to the poverty line:

- A family membership at the YMCA in Des Moines, IA costs $82 per month.
- Group lessons for swimming instruction in New York City run upwards of $45 per class.
- Soccer classes in Sacramento, CA cost approximately $150 for an 8-week session of instruction.
- Golf lessons in Austin, TX begin at a $150 for a 12-week course through organizations dedicated to making sports more widely available. At more exclusive locations, the lessons can begin at $75–$100 for individual instruction.
- As an organization, Little League is technically a non-profit entity but there are costs associated with joining the teams. The fees range nationwide from $50–$200 for a season of play.

These costs illustrate the challenge of adding sports and physical activity into a family budget that is below the median level reported by the U.S. Census. And while some of the programs listed above offer low-cost ways for children to engage in athletic activities, there are usually ancillary costs (such as uniforms and travel) that are associated with these activities. It is important to note that a number of programs and organizations provide free athletic opportunities to young children including: the Boys and Girls Club, various State Departments of Parks and Recreation, and the Fresh Air Fund, to name a selection. These programs are important assets to the communities they serve. Interestingly, there are a number of sports and athletic charities that provide access to athletics and training for sports to disadvantaged children globally rather than locally, providing a fruitful area of redress for scholars and activists interested in athletic equity nationwide.

Theorizing the Effects of Inequalities

Given the differences in access and experience to athletic and sporting activities for different groups of children, one can reasonably wonder, what are the effects of these differences? What are the consequences of various groups of children growing up with different levels of access?

Perpetuating Cycles of Privilege

The term *war on poverty* gathered steam in the 1960s in response to what is commonly known as the Moynihan Report, a commentary written by Daniel Patrick Moynihan under the presidency of Lyndon Johnson. This report explored the root causes of poverty in the African-American community and determined, controversially, that African-American families were not able to achieve economic, political, or social justice because of high rates of single motherhood in the African-American community. This report fueled a restrictive and deficit-oriented rhetoric around *cycles of poverty*, a concept that references a perceived phenomenon in which poor families become and remain impoverished through generations. More than 50 years later, we can still see evidence of this discourse in contemporary media featuring young families of color who are unable to "lift" themselves out of poverty and forge new paths.

The problem with this thinking, as critical scholars have noted (see Banks, 2004; Ladson-Billings, 2009; West, 1993), is that it relies on an assumption that those with fewer resources are the sole architects of their life circumstances, and it ignores, for example, the numerous institutional structures that impede economic, political, and social justice for families who have been marginalized because of race, class, sexual orientation, and dis/ability, among other factors. The intersection of the rhetoric around *cycles of poverty* and athletics is important because access to—and engagement with—sports illustrates the very opposite of poverty: that is, privilege. Families with financial means can buy access to sport and athletic opportunities in ways that families experiencing poverty cannot. Cementing access to athletics for young children is a way to sustain privilege. In other words, children with access to high-quality sports, athletics, and physical activity are children whose parents can afford these opportunities for them. It is an element of financial and social privilege that is conferred upon the few, rather than the many. Without a committed effort to offer these opportunities to children of all economic, racial, social, and ability backgrounds, a cycle of privilege is maintained wherein children with means continue to partake of activities that are not available to all.

This chapter takes an initial look at the inequalities with regard to physical and sporting activities for young children. While it is beyond the scope of the chapter to investigate all of the important intersections with regard to sports and athletics, it is nonetheless important to provide thoughtful investigation and analysis in these areas. Future inquiry could and should analyze the ways in which equality in athletics for young children is affected by race, class, gender, poverty, and dis/ability. While this list is not comprehensive, it represents some of the ways in which access is restricted for some children and some families, and maintained for those who have the means to acquire access.

Recommendations

This chapter concludes with a set of recommendations for addressing inequalities for young children with regards to physical activity and physical education. While it is impossible to put forth a series of recommendations that will solve the problems of access, it is also neglectful to ignore possibilities for reducing these inequalities. By this point, the reader will note that the issues concerning access to physical activity and education for young children are greater than discrete concerns over facilities, equipment, instructors, and the like. Rather, the concerns are broader and more comprehensive, mirroring persistent issues of inequality and unfairness in our society. These recommendations, therefore, call for a more expansive approach to the issues at hand.

- *Physical activities should be varied and evenly distributed.* Actually achieving this requires investments in communities in a number of ways including, but not limited to, affordable housing, quality childcare, and healthful, affordable food. Addressing access to physical activity and education requires a larger-scale understanding of the forces that limit or inhibit access to physical activities for families all across the country. This includes access to clean, safe parks; adequate employment as well as adequate time spent away from work; and access to affordable, healthful food. Addressing the narrower issues of access to physical activity and education requires a willingness to address larger and more systemic inequalities facing young children and their families, including poverty and housing.
- *Standardized testing should be rethought so that curriculum narrowing is not a common outcome.* Rather than eliminate the important time for recess and physical education, schools should be encouraged—perhaps even required!—to find ways to increase the amount of time children spend on drama, art, creative play, dance, sports, technology, gym, coding, movement, public speaking, and the like. Researchers and practitioners are overwhelmingly in support of children having the time and space in their school and pre-school day to engage in and enjoy these activities. Parents and children are also supportive. With everyone on board, why is

it so hard to make it happen? The forces behind standardized testing and accountability movements are fairly strong, and they require an equally strong force in opposition in order to gain any traction. It is incumbent on educators, researchers, parents, administrators, and citizens at large to mount thoughtful and serious challenges to the standardized testing movement, and in so doing, demand that our young children have inviolable time set aside for creative play and physical activity.

- *Reduce screen time and increase physical activity.* The advent of screens in our lives has created robust opportunities for connection, engagement, and information-sharing. It has also drastically decreased the number of minutes adults and children spend being active and interacting with other humans. Reducing screen time in young children is an important and common-sense method of increasing movement and activity. Yet, it is equally important to explore and understand the socio-demographic factors that influence a caregiver's decision to green-light screen time, such as a lack of affordable childcare. A broader understanding of these factors would set the stage for an intervention aimed at reducing screen time and increasing healthy activity.
- *Embrace and exhibit broader support for community programs such as the YMCA and national programs such as the Let's Move! campaign.* Comprehensive support for programs that address childhood obesity and physical activity through community initiatives requires a robust level of commitment from citizens across all socio-demographic sectors. It is easy—and common—for individuals to support programs and initiatives that directly influence or benefit them. For those among us who have adequate access to childcare, employment, affordable housing, public parks, gym facilities, and equipment, the need for public programs feels removed at best, and unnecessary at worst. To the contrary, it is important to shore up support for programs that encourage movement and active lifestyles across a broad spectrum of families and individuals.

References

Allendar, S., Cowburn, G., & Foster, C. (2006). Understanding participation in sport and physical activity among children and adults: A review of qualitative studies. *Health Education Research*, 21(6), 826–835.

Anderson, S. E., Economos, C. D., & Must, A. (2008). Active play and screen time in US children aged 4 to 11 years in relation to sociodemographic and weight status characteristics: A nationally representative cross-sectional analysis. *BMC Public Health*, 8(1), 366.

Banks, J. A. (2004). Multicultural education: Historical development, dimensions, and practice. In J. A. Banks (Ed.), *Handbook of research on multicultural education* (2nd ed., pp. 3–30). San Francisco, CA: Jossey-Bass.

Berliner, D. (2011). Rational responses to high stakes testing: The case of curriculum narrowing and the harm that follows. *Cambridge Journal of Education*, 41(3), 287–302.

Burdette, H. L., & Whitaker, R. C. (2005). Resurrecting free play in young children: Looking beyond fitness and fatness to attention, affiliation, and affect. *Archives of Pediatric and Adolescent Medicine, 159*(1), 46–50.

Carlson, S. A., Fulton, J. E., Lee, S. M., Maynard, L. M., Brown, D. R., Kohl, H. W., & Dietz, W. H. (2008). Physical education and academic achievement in elementary school: Data from the early childhood longitudinal study. *American Journal of Public Health, 98*(4), 721–727.

Carson, V., Rosu, A., & Janssen, I. (2014). A cross-sectional study of the environment, physical activity, and screen time among young children and their parents. *BMC Public Health, 14*(1), 61. doi:10.1186/1471-2458-14-61.

Cheung, P. C., Cunningham, S. A., Narayan, K. M. V., & Kramer, M. R. (2016). Childhood obesity incidence in the United States: A systematic review. *Childhood Obesity, 12*(1), 1–11.

Fernandes, M., & Sturm, R. (2010). Facility provision in elementary schools: Correlates with physical education, recess, and obesity. *Preventative Medicine, 50,* 30–35.

Hinkley, T., Salmon, J., Okely, A. D., Crawford, D., & Hesketh, K. (2012). Preschoolers' physical activity, screen time, and compliance with recommendations. *Medicine and Science in Sports and Exercise, 44*(3), 458–465.

Janssen, I., & LeBlanc, A. G. (2010). Systematic review of the health benefits of physical activity and fitness in school-aged children and youth. *International Journal of Behavioral Nutrition and Physical Activity, 7*(40), 1–16.

Jarrett, O. S. (2002). Recess in elementary school: What does the research say? *ERIC Digest,* 1–7. doi:http://files.eric.ed.gov/fulltext/ED466331.pdf.

Johnson, D. D., & Johnson, B. (2006). *High stakes: Poverty, testing, and failure in American schools* (2nd ed.). Oxford, UK: Rowman & Littlefield Publishers, Inc.

Kozol, J. (1991). *Savage inequalities: Children in America's schools.* New York: Harper Collins Publishers, Inc.

Ladson-Billings, G. (2009). *The dreamkeepers: Successful teachers of African-American children* (2nd ed.). San Francisco, CA: Jossey-Bass.

McKenzie, T. L., & Kahan, D. (2008). Physical activity, public health, and elementary schools. *The Elementary School Journal, 108*(3), 171–180.

Ogden, C. L., Carroll, M. D., Lawman, H. G., Fryar, C. D., Kruszon-Moran, D., Kit, B. K., & Flegal, K. M. (2016). Trends in obesity prevalence among children and adolescents in the United States, 1988–1994 through 2013–2014. *JAMA: Journal of the American Medical Association, 315*(21), 2292–2299.

Ohanian, S. (2002). *What happened to recess and why are our children struggling in kindergarten?* New York: The McGraw-Hill Companies, Inc.

Ramstetter, C. L., Murray, R., & Garner, A. S. (2010). The crucial role of recess in schools. *School Health, 80*(11), 517–526.

Stork, S., & Sanders, S. W. (2008). Physical education in early childhood. *The Elementary School Journal, 108*(3), 198–206.

West, C. (1993). *Race matters.* Boston, MA: Beacon Press.

Xu, H., Wen, L. M., & Rissel, C. (2015). Associations of parental influences with physical activity and screen time among young children: A systematic review. *Journal of Obesity.* doi:dx.doi.org/10.1155/2015/546925.

10 Life Sciences

Reaching for the Stars from the Start: Early Learning Experiences in the Sciences

Nancy P. Morabito

Introduction

> Every kid starts out as a natural-born scientist, and then we beat it out of them. A few trickle through the system with their wonder and enthusiasm for science intact.
>
> (Carl Sagan, in an interview with *Psychology Today*;
> Anonymous, 1996)

Although the metaphor of children acting as scientists may be imperfect (Kuhn, 1989), through this quotation, scientist and author Carl Sagan raised two important points: (1) the significance of children's inherent curiosity; and (2) the lack of sustained support of such curiosity in some educational settings. While the cultivation of an appreciation of science is the responsibility of educators across all grade levels, it is particularly important that teachers of very young children draw upon their students' curiosity in order to lay the groundwork for a life full of "wonder and enthusiasm for science." While there are certainly numerous high-quality schools and programs in existence that effectively support young learners, as Darling-Hammond (2013) pointed out:

> Many children do not have the kinds of experiences at home or in a preschool that allow them to develop the communication and inter-action skills, motor skills, social-emotional skills, and cognitive skills that are required for them to be independent learners when they start school, which undermines their academic success in both the short and the longer run.
>
> (pp. 80–81)

One might argue that, in addition to the skills identified by Darling-Hammond, numerous young children may also lack experiences that foster their natural curiosity about the world around them, which may impact their interest in and enthusiasm for science-related instruction throughout their lives. As has been addressed in various contexts elsewhere in this book, the effects of poverty play an important role in the different types of learning experiences made available to children in their early years. This chapter, therefore, considers the particular impact of such inequalities on science teaching and learning by exploring the current landscape of early childhood science education, considering the potential impacts of poverty on such education, and then focusing largely on opportunities and challenges ahead as we work to support students' curiosity about the world around them.

Science During the Early Childhood Years

As noted in *A Framework for K-12 Science Education: Practices, Crosscutting Concepts, and Core Ideas* (National Research Council [NRC], 2012), "A rich science education has the potential to capture students' sense of wonder about the world and to spark their desire to continue learning about science throughout their lives" (p. 28). Accordingly, in its position statement on early childhood science education, the National Science Teachers Association ([NSTA], 2014) calls for the engagement of young children in science learning in order to lay the groundwork for successful learning in elementary school and beyond. Furthermore, recent reform efforts in science education borne out through the creation of reports such as *Taking Science to School: Learning and Teaching Science in Grades K-8* (NRC, 2007) and, more recently, the development of the *Framework-based Next Generation Science Standards* ([NGSS]; NGSS Lead States, 2013) reflect an increased emphasis on "learning that connects the 'what' of science with the 'how' and 'why'" (Duschl, Bismack, Greeno, & Gitomer, 2016, p. 5) in that they "recommend that science learning be organized around select conceptual knowledge frameworks and practices that, in turn, are coordinated around core content and learning progressions" (Duschl et al., 2016, p. 10). Although these reports and documents focus on learners in kindergarten and beyond, this increased focus on conceptual learning through engagement in the practices of science would seem, on some level, to lend itself naturally to enriching the inquiry-based learning experiences of even the youngest of children for whom learning through interaction with the world is so essential.

Young Children's Readiness for Science

While previous understandings of child development may have suggested that the types of learning espoused by these reform efforts may not be suitable for very young children, more recent research has challenged that perspective. Children are, in fact, much better equipped for science and inquiry-based learning than formerly believed, even at young ages (Metz, 1995, 1997). As Gelman and Brenneman (2004) stated:

> The last several decades of developmental research have resulted in the recognition that preschool children have some potent cognitive

competencies and related learning potentials. These include early arithmetic abilities and skills, implicit understanding of cause and effect sequences, pre-literacy "writing," and some science knowledge.

(p. 150)

This reframing of the abilities of young children highlights important opportunities for involving these students in meaningful science learning experiences early in their lives. Eshach and Fried (2005) further underscored the importance of early science learning experiences when they noted that not only do young children already possess this natural interest in the world, but also that, "on the other hand, children are in danger of losing their interest and their sense of wonder if we fail to tend to them and nourish them in this regard" (p. 320). By drawing upon the emerging science knowledge of these young learners to help them explore related content and practices, early childhood educators may nurture the seeds of curiosity and wonder that are already growing within their students.

Recent Science Initiatives and Early Childhood Education

Fortunately, the priorities of the initiatives put forth in documents such as the NGSS and by the NSTA align favorably with recent shifts in understanding of what is considered appropriate and manageable for young children. That is, fostering early conceptual understanding of the world through engagement in the practices of science is not beyond the capabilities of these young learners. According to Eshach and Fried (2005), "[t]he pleasure children take in nature, in playing, in collecting, in observing, make them, in this way, temperamentally ready not only for the things of science but also for first steps toward the ideas of science" (pp. 319–320). Drawing upon the important aspects of discovery through play and experience with the natural world, in conjunction with what sparks students' innate curiosity and interests (e.g., Johnson, Alexander, Spencer, Leibham, & Neitzel, 2004), is fundamental to the development of such meaningful learning experiences. Ultimately, providing such learning experiences will support young learners in their future development of conceptual understanding and engagement with the practices of science as advocated by the NGSS.

Inequalities in (Early) Education

As has been discussed elsewhere in this text, the inequities associated with poverty cast ripples of effects across multiple aspects of a child's life. For instance, young children's (in)ability to engage in play alone, due to a lack of resources/ equipment (e.g., playgrounds) or safety concerns when living in poverty, has dire consequences for their future physical and social-emotional development (Milteer, Ginsburg, Council on Communications and Media Committee on Psychosocial Aspects of Child and Family Health, & Mulligan, 2012).

With respect to formal school settings, consider the student population and educational environment faced by some teachers around the nation working in impoverished settings. For example, Jonathan Kozol's (1991) well-known work, *Savage Inequalities*, documented the abysmal conditions found in under-privileged schools that he visited around the nation. For a more in-depth, insider exploration of the conditions facing such disadvantaged schools, Johnson and Johnson (2006) returned to an elementary school classroom for a year in a brutally under-resourced school and community. Of their students, they stated that, "[m]any of the children . . . are the poorest of the poor. Their homes are substandard and include trailers, shotgun houses, and housing pro-ject apartments. Some lack electricity and running water . . . Many of the children do not receive medical or dental care" (p. xv). With respect to the school facilities themselves, which were originally built in 1948, Johnson and Johnson described:

> The floors showed over a half century of filth waxed over annu-ally . . . The windows, tops of the fluorescent lights, and rickety ceiling fans looked as if they had never been cleaned. Apparently, the walls had not been painted since the construction of the school. Scuff marks, holes, cracks, tape, falling plaster, and other signs of neglect were eve-rywhere . . . [in one classroom] a hole offered a view into the next classroom. In both rooms, the poor fit of the wheezing window air conditioners allowed daylight to come in around the units . . . The rooms and hallways had the smell of age—mildew and decades of accumulated dirt.
>
> (p. 5)

Additional anecdotes in the book describe myriad problems including, but not limited to, vermin infestations, severely outdated encyclopedias and textbooks, dire life circumstances for students (e.g., lack of food, inability to address medical and dental issues, loss of homes), freezing cold class-rooms during winter months, and the pressures exerted upon teachers by the high-stakes tests to which their students are subjected (and subsequently compared to students in better-funded schools and districts).

Although many researchers, including Johnson and Johnson (2006), have called into question the measures used to assess student achievement by identifying the inherent biases of such instruments, overall, research has shown that high-quality early childhood learning experiences can help narrow the achievement gap between populations of students of varying socioeconomic statuses (Barnett & Lamy, 2013). Barnett and Lamy, how-ever, also pointed out a notable "opportunity gap in access to high-quality early learning programs to families across the country" (p. 105). These authors noted that, while certain programs have been put in place to help address these disparities (e.g., Early Head Start), more widespread efforts are needed.

Given the focus of this chapter on science education in particular, it is also worth noting that the science materials Johnson and Johnson (2006) found in one classroom "consisted of a dusty beaker and a cardboard box of rocks, labeled *Rocks*. Some of the rocks and most of the labels were missing" (p. 6). Although these (and other) authors' experiences took place in elementary, middle, and high schools rather than early childhood settings, their descriptions of such sub-optimal home and learning environments beg the question: With the ongoing push for the engagement of students in meaningful science learning experiences as described previously, how might one even begin to imagine conducting such instruction given these types of circumstances? While it is, perhaps, not so difficult to envision the form of instruction for which the NGSS and other science education reform movements advocate occurring in well-funded schools with an abundance of (or even simply adequate) resources, it is infinitely more difficult to determine where to start in the dire settings described by Johnson and Johnson, Kozol, and others.

Opportunities and Challenges for Early Science Education in Under-Resourced Schools

Based on the shifting perspective on the readiness of young children to participate in science learning, and because of the changing priorities in science education described previously, multiple curricula have been developed to engage young learners with science content and thinking. For example, the Preschool Pathways to Science curriculum ([PrePS], Gelman & Brenneman, 2004) "creates an environment of conceptually connected learning experiences that supports a curious intellectual attitude and movement along relevant learning paths" (p. 156). This curriculum strives to engage young children with science practices such as observation and prediction, address core science concepts (e.g., biological change), and create connections to other disciplines such as literacy and mathematics. Likewise, the ScienceStart! Curriculum (French, 2004) aims to draw upon

> preschoolers' fascination with learning about the everyday world as the starting point for planned/structured activities that are designed to foster . . . development in the areas of language, early literacy, attention regulation, planning, and problem solving . . . [through] sustained, coherent investigations of natural phenomena.
>
> (p. 139)

In addition to these comprehensive curricula, resources for more standalone activities and/or units of study abound as well. While some of these activities focus on outdoor, nature-based exploration (e.g., Shaffer, Hall, & Lynch, 2009; Sisson & Lash, 2017), others are designed to take place primarily within a classroom setting (e.g., Hachey & Butler, 2009; Hoisington,

Chalufour, Winokur, & Clark-Chiarelli, 2014; Trundle & Sackes, 2008). Often these classroom-based activities and units of study rely on the use of learning centers and/or sensory tables for exploration of different aspects of the phenomena under investigation. For instance, Hachey and Butler's (2009) description of students' exploration of nature through gardening suggests the use of sensory tables to provide young children with the opportunity to play with soil and gardening tools, as well as "a variety of rocks, high-quality plastic insect models, and a handful of seeds" (p. 46).

However, as can be imagined based on the descriptions of severely under-resourced schools provided by researchers and authors such as Johnson and Johnson (2006), not all schools have the material resources to support such experiences (e.g., sensory tables), and nor do all schools exist in and/or families live in environments that are conducive to low-cost exploration outside the home (e.g., safety concerns related to going outside to observe trees during the day and/or the moon at night). Indeed, contributors to *Taking Science to School* acknowledged the need for further investigation of "the systemic issues that contribute to inequities in science education" and "that inequities in the quality of instruction, the qualifications of teachers, resources, facilities, and time devoted to science are unacceptable and must be addressed" (NRC, 2007, p. 347). This report then called for revision of school- and district-level policies in order to mitigate such inequalities.

When considering the potential impacts of these policy shifts, it is important to remain aware that the teaching and learning that occurs in classrooms does not always reflect or align with the learning and instruction outlined in curricular guides/guidelines (e.g., science learning standards) (Brickhouse, 2016). Brickhouse further pointed out that,

> [t]he challenge with achieving educational equity by focusing on the improvement of standards . . . is that schooling occurs in a place . . . The local communities in which schools are embedded must not only embrace the educational aims of science education, they must be able to articulate them in ways that speak to the needs and goals of particular communities.
>
> (p. 234)

This applies not only to learning and instruction for older children, but for young students as well.

Some early childhood curricula that incorporate science instruction strive to address these issues, specifically focusing on the needs of under-resourced communities and schools in order to support high-quality instruction in early childhood learning settings. For instance, the Connect4Learning curriculum aims to address these needs by "leading with math and science content, supporting social-emotional development, narrowing the vocabulary gap, and broadening children's horizons" (Connect4Learning, 2015, p. 12). However, for those schools who do not have access to such curricula and/or the material resources needed to implement them fully, it is important to consider how students may still engage in meaningful science-related experiences.

In order to begin immersing young learners in the practices of science while also laying a foundation for conceptual understanding, one particular practice is of paramount importance: observation. As Eberbach and Crowley (2009) have noted, observation underlies all scientific activity. However, although children are constantly observing the world around them as "everyday observers," early childhood educators (and all science educators, for that matter) need to cultivate children's scientific observation skills. That is, rather than assume that students will naturally attend to the important features of the observed phenomenon, they must be guided to act as "scientific observers" (Eberbach & Crowley, 2009). Such preparation is needed in order to foster connections to science concepts and content. In describing a study of one particular curriculum that emphasized observations of birds, Eberbach and Crowley (2009) provided the following example demonstrating the need for attention to scientific observation skills:

> Evaluation suggested that the [curriculum] developers—who included educators and expert ornithologists—had underestimated the complexity of observational practice, its interrelationship with disciplinary knowledge, and the degree to which teachers and students needed scaffolding to support systematic observation. Like so many, they had assumed it is easy to observe birds. Yet, problems with identifying and counting birds soon emerged:
> Students could not identify birds in flight, nor could they distinguish between individual birds, making it impossible to generate accurate population counts. As trained observers, ornithologists know what features to observe when identifying kinds of birds and to look for field marks to identify individual birds in flight. Lacking this specialized knowledge and practice, students were unable to make scientifically meaningful observations.
>
> (p. 40)

These authors then went on to characterize the types of observations made by these students as everyday observations rather than scientific, noting that scientific observation is more systematic in nature than everyday observation. Four components of scientific observation were then identified: noticing phenomena, expectations about such phenomena, observational records, and productive dispositions (p. 47).

Although the students who engaged in the bird observation curriculum described by Eberbach and Crowley (2009) were in middle school, the support for children as they transition from everyday observers to scientific observers can begin in early childhood. The authors pointed out that, while their review of existing literature may indicate that children's observations generally are not scientific in nature, "children can indeed observe more scientifically when they learn in contexts that reflect disciplinary practice and support trajectories that connect their everyday observations with disciplinary knowledge" (p. 53). They also stressed the importance of students' learning how to record their observations based on guidance and instruction from their teachers.

The Importance of Observation in Under-Resourced Schools

Considering the challenges posed in under-resourced communities and schools (Milteer et al., 2012) in conjunction with the importance of and opportunities for observation as described by Eberbach and Crowley (2009), three major factors emerge to be addressed for young learners: safety, opportunities for observation, and means for recording observations. Fortunately for under-resourced schools, observation itself does not necessarily require significant material resources and can take place within the safety of a classroom. Although the means by which students can record their observations may be constrained by inequities in material resources, as well as young learners' emergent language and pre-writing skills, educators may consider ways to elicit students' observations and thinking that overcome such boundaries.

One example of an activity that can support young children's scientific observation skills is that of a leaf study. Students can explore leaf structure using several different samples collected by the teacher (or, safety and availability permitting, by students themselves) within the classroom. While observing, young children can create leaf rubbings and/or generate their own representations of the leaves using relatively low-cost materials (e.g., paper and crayons). In order to learn more about the child's thinking about the leaves under observation, students may describe the leaves and/or what is revealed through the leaf rubbings verbally to the teacher. This would allow the teacher to guide their students to refine their observation skills (e.g., calling attention to particular features of different leaf samples), record children's thinking, and probe for further explanation for the students' statements. These conversations could also indicate what related disciplinary content might be of interest to the students for further exploration in the future.

Conclusion

Returning to the quotation from Carl Sagan included at the beginning of this chapter, educators of children of all ages should aspire to support their students in maintaining their "wonder and enthusiasm for science" rather than "beat it out of them" (as cited in Anonymous, 1996). One practice that may help cultivate such curiosity in young children, even in under-resourced settings, is that of observation. Unfortunately, as Eberbach and Crowley (2009) noted:

When children are cast into an activity with inadequate knowledge and instructional support, observation becomes a weak method for collecting data rather than a powerful method for reasoning scientifically. In short, everyday observers fail to notice the right things. Instead, they notice many irrelevant features and behaviors that fail to forge connections or to support deeper understanding of complex phenomena. Disciplinary knowledge, however, can filter, focus, and foster understanding.

(p. 49)

Disciplinary knowledge is also important for beginning to understand what types of information should be recorded (p. 53). Therefore, young children must also have access to disciplinary knowledge to foster their scientific observation skills, and obtaining these resources can be more challenging for under-resourced schools. Eberbach and Crowley further emphasized the role of the learning environment in supporting students as they transition to more scientific observers. Recalling the classroom conditions described by Johnson and Johnson (2006) earlier in this chapter, it is clear this may prove particularly challenging for under-resourced schools, as their learning environments are often sub-optimal.

These challenges speak to the call made in *Taking Science to School*, which charged the educational research community to account for the inequities that exist across learning environments for children of all ages, as well as develop and enact policies to address such inequalities (NRC, 2007). As this report noted,

all students bring . . . personal knowledge of the natural world, and curiosity, which can be built on . . . Adjusting for variation in students' background and experience does *not* mean dumbing down the science curriculum or instruction provided to certain groups of students.

(p. 340, emphasis added)

Therefore, it is our responsibility to ensure that children of all ages are not beaten down with respect to science, but instead are encouraged to reach for the stars.

References

Anonymous. (1996). A slayer of demons. *Psychology Today, 29*(1), 30–33.
Barnett, W. S., & Lamy, C. E. (2013). Achievement gaps start early: Preschool can help. In P. L. Carter & K. G. Welner (Eds.), *Closing the opportunity gap: What America must do to give every child an even chance* (pp. 98–110). New York: Oxford.
Brickhouse, N. (2016). Views from above and below: Access to science education. In R. A. Duschl & A. S. Bismack (Eds.), *Reconceptualizing STEM education: The central role of practices* (pp. 232–236). New York: Routledge.

Connect4Learning. (2015). *The pre-K curriculum: Addressing the needs of children from underresourced communities.* Retrieved from www.connect4learning.com.

Darling-Hammond, L. (2013). Inequality and school resources: What it will take to close the opportunity gap. In P. L. Carter & K. G. Welner (Eds.), *Closing the opportunity gap: What America must do to give every child an even chance* (pp. 77–97). New York: Oxford.

Duschl, R. A., Bismack, A. S., Greeno, J., & Gitomer, D. H. (2016). Introduction: Coordinating pre-K-16 STEM education research and practices for advancing and refining reform agendas. In R. A. Duschl & A. S. Bismack (Eds.), *Reconceptualizing STEM education: The central role of practices* (pp. 1–32). New York: Routledge.

Eberbach, C., & Crowley, K. (2009). From everyday to scientific observation: How children learn to observe the biologist's world. *Review of Educational Research, 79*(1), 39–68.

Eshach, H., & Fried, M. N. (2005). Should science be taught in early childhood? *Journal of Science Education and Technology, 14*(3), 315–336.

French, L. (2004). Science as the center of a coherent, integrated early childhood curriculum. *Early Childhood Research Quarterly, 19*, 138–149.

Gelman, R., & Brenneman, K. (2004). Science learning pathways for young children. *Early Childhood Research Quarterly, 19*, 150–158.

Hachey, A. C., & Butler, D. L. (2009). Seeds in the window, soil in the sensory table: Science education through gardening and nature-based play. *Young Children, 64*(6), 42–48.

Hoisington, C., Chalufour, I., Winokur, J., & Clark-Chiarelli, N. (2014). Promoting children's science inquiry and learning through water investigations. *Young Children, 69*(4), 72–79.

Johnson, D. D., & Johnson, B. (2006). *High stakes: Poverty, testing, and failure in American schools* (2nd ed.). Lanham, MD: Rowman & Littlefield.

Johnson, K. E., Alexander, J. M., Spencer, S., Leibham, M. E., & Neitzel, C. (2004). Factors associated with the early emergence of intense interests within conceptual domains. *Cognitive Development, 19*, 325–343.

Kozol, J. (1991). *Savage inequalities: Children in America's schools.* New York: Random House.

Kuhn, D. (1989). Children and adults as intuitive scientists. *Psychological Review, 96*(4), 674–689.

Metz, K. E. (1995). Reassessment of developmental constraints on children's science instruction. *Review of Educational Research, 65*(2), 93–127.

Metz, K. E. (1997). On the complex relation between cognitive developmental research and children's science curricula. *Review of Educational Research, 67*(1), 151–163.

Milteer, R. M., Ginsburg, K. R., Council on Communications and Media Committee on Psychosocial Aspects of Child and Family Health, & Mulligan, D. A. (2012). The importance of play in promoting healthy child development and maintaining strong parent-child bond: Focus on children in poverty. *Pediatrics, 129*(1), e204–e213.

National Research Council. (2007). *Taking science to school: Learning and teaching science in grades K-8.* Washington, DC: National Academies Press.

National Research Council. (2012). *A framework for K-12 science education: Practices, crosscutting concepts, and core ideas.* Washington, D.C.: National Academies Press.

National Science Teachers Association. (2014). *NSTA position statement: Early childhood science education*. Arlington, VA: NSTA.

NGSS Lead States. (2013). *Next generation science standards: For states, by states*. Washington, D.C.: National Academies Press.

Shaffer, L. F., Hall, E., & Lynch, M. (2009). Toddlers' scientific explorations: Encounters with insects. *Young Children, 64*(6), 18–23.

Sisson, J. H., & Lash, M. (2017). Outdoor learning experiences connecting children to nature: Perspectives from Australia and the United States. *Young Children, 72*(4), 8–16.

Trundle, K. C., & Sackes, M. (2008). Sky observation by the book: Lessons for teaching young children astronomy concepts with picture books. *Science and Children, 46*(1), 36–39.

11 Earth Sciences and Geography

How Geographic Settings Contribute to Child Poverty with Implications for Child Citizenship Development

Donald R. McClure

Child poverty is a critical issue for our time. Societies are often judged by the way they care for their most vulnerable citizens, and children living in poverty—young people who lack even the most basic resources to live safely and in good health—are among the most vulnerable of citizens today. As the U.S. Department of Commerce, U.S. Census Bureau (2016), reported,

> For children under age 18 [in the US], 19.7 percent and 14.5 million were in poverty in 2015, down from 21.1 percent and 15.5 million in 2014. Children represented 23.1 percent of the total population in 2015 and 33.6 percent of the people in poverty.
>
> (p. 14)

Child poverty, however, is not only a U.S. problem; it is a worldwide problem. A collaborative research study between UNICEF and the World Bank Group (2016) reported that an estimated 385 million children between the ages of 0 and 17 who lived in 89 countries around the globe (countries accounting for approximately 84 percent of the total population of residents in developing countries) lived in extreme poverty. Extreme poverty was defined as a person living on welfare of $1.90 or less per day. The study noted that these impoverished children were heavily concentrated in Sub-Saharan Africa and South Asia. The report stated, "The consequences of inadequate nutrition, a lack of early stimulation and learning, and exposure to stress last a lifetime" (UNICEF & World Bank Group, 2016, p. 2).

This chapter answers the question, "How do geographic settings contribute to child poverty?" UNICEF's (2004) statement of "children in poverty" identified three resource deprivations that children in poverty could encounter: material, spiritual, and emotional. In this chapter, these three deprivations are used as a framework to understand three separate cases of child poverty in the United States, Ireland, and Nigeria. The chapter also examines how geographic settings in these contexts contributed to child poverty and concludes with some implications for child citizenship development.

What Is Child Poverty? Material, Spiritual, and Emotional Resource Deprivation

Although different conceptualizations of child poverty exist, this chapter uses UNICEF's (2004) understanding of "children in poverty" as a framework for analysis:

> Children living in poverty experience deprivation of the material, spiritual, and emotional resources needed to survive, develop and thrive, leaving them unable to enjoy their rights, achieve their full potential or participate as full and equal members of society.
>
> (UNICEF, 2004, p. 18)

Material resources, the first deprivation, refer to "income, food, access to education or health service, [and] protection from health risks, such as those associated with hard physical work and others" (UNICEF, 2007, p. 7). Spiritual resources are described as "stimuli, meaningfulness, expectations, role models, and peer relationships, and emotional resources include love, trust, feelings of acceptance, inclusion, and lack of abusive situations" (UNICEF, 2007, p. 7). These deprivations can overlap in children's lives and have long-lasting effects on their futures. Furthermore, children in both rich and poor countries alike can experience these three poverty deprivations. "On average, low-income countries tend to have higher rates of deprivation than middle-income countries. Yet a significant number of children in middle-income countries are still exposed to severe deprivations" (UNICEF, 2004, p. 23). UNICEF has also noted that discrimination based on gender can significantly influence child poverty.

Material Resource Deprivation: The Water Crisis in Flint, Michigan, USA

In April 2014, the city of Flint, Michigan experienced a water crisis that put the health and safety of its residents, particularly its children, at great risk. Before the crisis began, an emergency manager was appointed by the State of Michigan to supervise Flint as the city worked to improve its financial standing. In an effort to cut costs, Flint changed its water source; however, this change ultimately endangered the city's residents. As Gray (2017, April 25) of the *Detroit Free Press* reported, the city

> switched its drinking water source from the Detroit Water and Sewage Department, which draws its water from Lake Huron, to the Flint River. The more-corrosive Flint River water was not treated with proper corrosion controls and caused lead to leach from pipes into homes and businesses.
>
> (para. 12)

Gray also reported that soon after the change, residents became alarmed because water coming from taps was discolored and odorous. In September 2015, over a year after the crisis began, the State of Michigan began providing bottled water and water filters to Flint residents.

There were many serious effects to Flint's water crisis. For example, General Motors announced in October 2014 that its factories would no longer use Flint water due to concerns over corrosion in its machinery (Kennedy, 2016, April 20). One of the most serious effects, however, concerned the health and safety of Flint's children—children who, in many cases, already came from impoverished backgrounds; in 2015, the Department of Commerce, U.S. Census Bureau estimated that approximately 40 percent of Flint's residents lived in poverty. The lead present in Flint's drinking water, which children could access in homes, schools, and other public places, posed a significant danger to the children. The U.S. Department of Health and Human Services, Centers for Disease Control and Prevention (CDC), for example, stated in its 2005 report *Preventing Lead Poisoning in Young Children* that lead poisoning in children is associated with health impairments such as reduced cognitive functioning and physical growth.

To determine what effect(s), if any, Flint's water crisis had on the blood lead levels of Flint's children, researchers Hanna-Attisha, LaChance, Sadler, and Champney Schnepp (2016) conducted a study to measure and compare the blood lead levels of children under five years of age in 2013 and again in 2015 in Greater Flint, Michigan. The researchers found that, "The percentage of children with elevated blood lead levels increased after water source change, particularly in socioeconomically disadvantaged neighborhoods" (p. 283). For children living outside Flint, however, Hanna-Attisha et al. did not observe any significant changes in blood lead levels. The researchers wrote, "Increased lead-poisoning rates have profound implications for the life course potential of an entire cohort of Flint children already rattled with toxic stress contributors (e.g., poverty, violence, unemployment, food insecurity)" (p. 286).

The Contribution of the Geographic Setting to Child Poverty

In the case of the Flint water crisis, the geographic setting of Flint had a strong influence on the material resource deprivation that the city's children experienced, particularly in terms of protection from health risks. For example, the children of Flint lived in a setting that experienced urban blight. This blight was influenced, in part, by Flint's aging infrastructure, including its inadequately maintained water treatment system, which caused lead to leach from pipes into the city's drinking water. In contrast, children and families who lived in more advantaged areas outside Flint were not exposed to health risks to the same degree as people living in Flint were, largely because suburban residents used infrastructure in their communities that was better maintained.

At least one reason for this contrast could be the result of policies enacted in the 1900s that led to Flint becoming a politically fragmented metropolitan area. As Sadler and Highsmith (2016) explained, in the early 1900s, many people from the South, especially African Americans, moved to Flint to fill jobs at General Motors factories. As the population of African Americans in Flint increased, many White people moved out of the city and began establishing suburbs.

> Once ensconced in their new communities, white suburbanites created new independent governments, resisted affiliations with Flint and its people—particularly African Americans and the poor—and insulated themselves from the urban economic crisis that ultimately precipitated the [Flint water crisis].
>
> (Sadler & Highsmith, 2016, p. 144)

In light of many Flint taxpayers moving to the suburbs over the course of several decades, coupled with legislation in Michigan in the late 1970s that prevented Flint from annexing suburban areas (called townships), the city's economy suffered and racial, social, and economic inequalities increased for children and families. The geographic setting of Flint, therefore, as well as political policies enacted over the years, contributed to how the residents of Flint, including children, experienced material resource deprivation and thus poverty.

Spiritual Resource Deprivation: Children of Nigerian Immigrants in the Republic of Ireland

In recent decades, a wave of new immigrants has arrived on Ireland's shores. Ireland's Central Statistics Office (CSO) (2017) reported, "In April 2016, persons born abroad accounted for 17.3 per cent of the population [in Ireland], up from 17 per cent in 2011" (p. 46). Today, there are over 810,000 residents in Ireland who were not born in the country out of a total population of nearly 4.8 million in the nation. Much of this change has occurred due to economic growth and expansion in the country. Although a large number of Ireland's current residents have come from countries inside the European Union (EU, a political body of which Ireland is a member), many people have come from countries outside the EU as well, including African nations such as Nigeria. As a result, diversity has increased in Ireland and has influenced Irish society in many ways.

This section introduces three children of Nigerian immigrants attending a primary school in Ireland and discusses how they experienced spiritual resource deprivation in terms of peer relationships. The section illustrates how the students' encounters with racism from White school-aged peers in their community led them to feel excluded, even though all three students were Irish-born and identified as Irish citizens. For a complete description of the research for this section, see McClure (2016).

Data were generated from September 2014 to December 2014 and May 2015 to June 2015 at St. Hilary School, a Catholic primary school in Lancaster, Ireland. (Pseudonyms are used for all place names and research participants in the study.) The three students, Candace, Victor, and Bella, were enrolled in the sixth grade. The students were also children of Nigerian immigrants and Irish citizens living in Lancaster. The children were born and raised in the Irish Republic.

The students' school and neighborhoods were located in a socially and economically disadvantaged area that experienced high rates of unemployment and drug and alcohol abuse. For example, St. Hilary itself was classified as a DEIS (Delivering Equality of Opportunity in Schools) band 1 school, meaning that the school encountered "impediments to education arising from social or economic disadvantage which prevent students from deriving appropriate benefit from education in schools" (Department of Education and Skills, 2005, p. 7).

Individual interviews with each student, group interviews with the students, individual interviews with St. Hilary teachers and administrators, and school observations were conducted. The interviews were audio recorded, transcribed, and thematically coded for analysis using Dedoose. School observations took place on the school's campus in locations such as classrooms and on the school playground. During these observations, field notes were gathered in a notebook or on a laptop computer to document social interactions taking place among people at the school. Validity was established by generating data from different sources to achieve triangulation, conducting regular debriefings with research scholars, monitoring subjectivity by analysis memos, and conducting member checks.

"If I Told How Much Racism I've Seen through My Life, It's Gonna Take a Week . . ."

In individual and group interviews with the students, the children reported that racism from White peers permeated much of their lives. The discrimination they experienced took place in locations such as the school playground and in their neighborhoods. For example, Candace, a sixth-grade student, once described discrimination she experienced by White children who also attended St. Hilary and lived next door to her. This experience took place outside school when Candace's White friend, Holly, visited Candace's house to play. Candace explained,

> Playing outside, if Holly came to knock for me and my neighbors are outside, they'd say to Holly, "Holly, you're playing with a Black girl!" and then Holly would stand up for me and then we'd leave.

You wouldn't play outside as much unless someone came to knock for you. Then you'd probably go. I wouldn't go outside if no one didn't knock for me.

Victor, also a sixth-grade student, described racism he experienced from White peers that intersected with his African background. The instance he shared below included discriminatory questions about the Ebola virus. Victor said,

> My dad was in Africa not long ago, and in that week, I have at least ten people coming up to me saying, "Does anyone in your family have Ebola?" And it's really an awkward question to answer. I'll be just like, "Go away." Like, and sometimes, I've just had to go away cause it just wrecks your head . . . when people come up to you with stupid questions like that.

Bella encountered racism on the school playground when White boys teased her about her hair braids. Regarding the boys, Bella said, "They call me, like, Bob Marley . . . I wear these braids every day now. If they say anything, they know in their heads it's not gonna work so then they just stop completely." Bella believed these kinds of discriminatory experiences occurred when teachers did not monitor student interactions as closely. Although teachers supervised students on the playground, these teachers also attended to multiple responsibilities and were not always fully aware of all interactions taking place among students who were spread out over a large area. Furthermore, as Bella's teacher, Mr. Malone, once explained in an interview,

> Usually, arguments won't take place when I'm in the classroom. It happens during a P.E. lesson or during a lunch break or something like that when there's a little bit more space and a bit more interaction between one another.

Therefore, when teachers did not monitor students as closely at St. Hilary, conflicts between students were more likely to occur.

The racism that Candace, Victor, and Bella experienced had harmful effects on the children. For example, Candace, a quiet and reserved girl, explained that she preferred to stay indoors and take up hobbies such as reading and drawing rather than go outside and risk possible confrontations with White peers. Candace once said she wanted to visit the public library to join a knitting club, but she chose not to because she was "just terrified to try to talk to the people. I wouldn't go on my own, just in case there's something racist." Bella and Victor said they had confrontations with White peers in the past. For example, in one group interview, Bella described a time when a White girl called her a discriminatory name. Bella said the name-calling led to a physical fight with the girl. Bella explained,

> I only ended up having a mark, but the other girl, she sprained her ankle. When I won, she was on the ground cryin' and I was like, "You say that to my face again and I swear to God, you won't make it through!"

In the same interview, Victor, who also recalled instances of being called discriminatory names based on the color of his skin, added that he had never lost a fight to a White person. He said, "I've never ever in my life lost a fight, and I've had so many." The spiritual resource deprivation the students experienced through racism from White peers had a strong effect on how they interacted with these peers in their community.

Overall, the experiences of discrimination that Candace, Victor, and Bella had made the children feel excluded in Lancaster. The children also felt as if they were not treated as full members of society in light of the racism they encountered. As Candace once put it in a group interview, "If I told how much racism I've seen through my life, it's gonna take a week . . ." (Bella and Victor agreed with Candace). Bella, Victor, and Candace experienced poverty in terms of spiritual resource deprivation through racism from White peers. Although Lancaster's status as an economically disadvantaged community likely influenced the children's experiences of inequality, this research suggests that the students' experiences of racism also had a strong influence on their lives. This racism was an added challenge to the economic inequalities that they and many of their White peers likely encountered in the community.

The Contribution of the Geographic Setting to Child Poverty

The geographic setting of the Irish Republic contributed to the students' experience of child poverty through spiritual resource deprivation. No doubt, Ireland has a long tradition of hospitality; for many years, people from different backgrounds and different parts of the world have travelled (and moved) to Ireland and have been warmly welcomed. However, as immigration and diversity have increased in Ireland in recent decades, researchers have argued that racism and anti-immigrant attitudes have also increased. For instance, Watson, Phádraig, Kennedy, and Rock–Huspatel (2007) reported that between 1995 and 2003, there was a rise in the number of Irish who believed immigrants were "associated with increased crime rates" and took "jobs away from people living in Ireland" (p. 219). Fanning (2002) argued that as far back as the 1990s, Black asylum seekers in Ireland were the victims of discrimination through racist propaganda. More recently, White (2012) argued that the media has played a role in perpetuating discrimination in Ireland through "a constant flow of racist representations and the counter-representations produced to challenge them" (p. 69).

Furthermore, at the primary school level, scholars of education in Ireland have documented incidents of discrimination among children in the midst of Ireland's demographic change. For example, Devine, Kenny, and Macneela (2008) reported that White primary schoolchildren used racist name-calling toward minority children both inside and outside school, and that sometimes this name-calling could intersect with immigrant students' countries of origin. The researchers also noted that name-calling at school took place "especially in the yard during playtime" (p. 375) when teachers' awareness of student interactions was limited. Other Irish educational scholarship has argued that discriminatory incidents have occurred between minority students and their Irish peers and teachers (Bryan, 2009; Devine, 2011; McClure, 2016). In the midst of increasing diversity in Ireland, the country has struggled with increased racism toward people from migrant communities—even in schools. It is notable, however, that there is evidence of progress. For example, education policies, such as the Intercultural Education Strategy for 2010–2015, have been released that aim to promote greater inclusion and diversity awareness in Irish schools. Regarding Candace's experience of racism from White peers that occurred in her own neighborhood (described earlier in this section), Candace's White friend, Holly, defended Candace. At St. Hilary, there were instances of teachers communicating inclusive messages to students, as well as students increasing their knowledge and understanding about people from diverse backgrounds. The St. Hilary school principal, Mr. O'Neal, explained, "I have deliberately set out here to create a culture in this school where the interactions between people . . . are characterized by friendliness and respect and courtesy." Although these are positive steps toward progress, children from an immigrant background at St. Hilary such as Candace, Victor, and Bella still experienced discrimination from White peers. In the context of a nation that is experiencing changing demographics and increased diversity, schools such as St. Hilary are struggling to create fully inclusive learning environments amidst a backdrop of larger societal inequalities. The geographic setting of Ireland and its existing social tensions, therefore, contributed to the experiences of racism (and thus child poverty) that Candace, Victor, and Bella encountered. In many instances, the three students were deprived of a vital spiritual resource—strong peer relationships—to help them thrive and "participate as full and equal members of society" (UNICEF, 2004, p. 18).

Emotional Resource Deprivation: The Abducted Schoolgirls in Nigeria

In April 2014, 276 girls attending a government secondary school in Chibok, a rural town in northeastern Nigeria, were kidnapped by the militant group Boko Haram. Elden (2014) defined Boko Haram as "a Sunni Islamist group, seeking to have Sharia (Islamic law) imposed in the north of Nigeria" (p. 414). Boko Haram began in the early 2000s and, for years, has been a vocal opponent of western education. The group's base "is in the north-eastern states of Yobe and Borno . . . close to Niger, Cameroon, and Chad" (Elden, 2014, p. 414).

This section argues that the kidnapped Nigerian schoolgirls encountered poverty through emotional resource deprivation. By drawing on news reports and extant research, the section concludes that the girls' kidnapping led to the students being deprived of inclusion, acceptance, and safety. It is important to note that economic circumstances likely played a role in the girls' experience of poverty as well. As Egiegba Agbiboa (2013) stated regarding socioeconomics in northern Nigeria,

> It is no coincidence that one of the worst forms of political violence in Nigeria today originates in the most socioeconomically deprived parts of the country. In the North, for example, where unemployment and chronic poverty are rife, radical Islamist groups have challenged the authority of the state.
>
> (p. 151)

Existing poverty in northern Nigeria, therefore, likely played a role in the emotional resource deprivation that the kidnapped schoolgirls encountered.

The Nigerian Girls' Kidnapping

Chibok is a town in Borno State in northeastern Nigeria. Because Chibok had not been the target of attacks by Boko Haram prior to April 14, 2014, local officials selected its government secondary school as the site for girls in the area to take final exams (Nigeria Chibok Abductions: What We Know, 2017, May 8). On the night of April 14, however, the attack on the school by Boko Haram militants took many by surprise and put the safety of the schoolgirls at risk.

Reports (Nigeria Chibok Abductions: What We Know, 2017, May 8; Okeowo, 2014, April 29; Sieff, 2016, April 14) contend that the militants entered the boarding school at night carrying guns. At first, the militants told the girls they had arrived to protect them. Soon, however, the girls saw the men stealing supplies from the school and setting fire to the school grounds. The militants abducted the girls and put them on vehicles to drive them away from Chibok. Initially, 276 girls were taken from the school, although dozens managed to escape in transit by jumping off vehicles and running to safety. In all, 219 schoolgirls who did not escape capture were abducted on April 14. As Chiluwa and Ifukor (2015) asserted, "By the kidnap of the Chibok schoolgirls, [Boko Haram] again demonstrated commitment to their philosophy of non-tolerance to western culture and influence, especially education for women and girls" (p. 268).

Following the abduction, confusion surfaced about the girls' whereabouts. There was disagreement about how many girls were taken and where the girls were. Okeowo (2014, April 29) reported,

> The day after the abduction, the Nigerian military claimed that it had rescued nearly all of the girls. A day later, the military retracted its claim; it had not actually rescued any of the girls. And the number that the government said was missing, just over a hundred, was less than half the number that parents and school officials counted: according to their tally, two hundred and thirty-four girls were taken.
>
> (para. 5)

Furthermore, many feared for the girls' safety. Peters (2014) claimed there were reports that the Boko Haram leader, Abubakar Shekau, intended to sell the girls. Chang (2016, April 27) reported that Boko Haram militants had a history of forcing women and girls "to marry Boko fighters and bear their children" (para. 8). Those who refused to marry the militants and have children could be killed. The missing schoolgirls' family members immediately began looking for the students, although no one, it seemed, was quite sure where the girls were. According to Peters (2014), reports claimed that the girls could have been transported across Nigeria's border to Chad and Cameroon.

After news broke about the abduction, people around the world reacted to the kidnappings. For example, Gordon Brown, the Special Envoy for Global Education at the United Nations, denounced the kidnappings, and President Barack Obama of the United States sent specialists to Africa to help the Nigerians look for the missing students (Peters, 2014). One of the most widespread responses to the kidnappings was the *#BringBackOurGirls* campaign on social media, especially on Twitter and Facebook. Chiluwa and Ifukor (2015) stated that the

> *#BringBackOurGirls* social media campaign with accompanying photographs and graphic images of children and schoolgirls on *Twitter* and *Facebook* was no longer a Nigerian affair; it became a global campaign for the release of the kidnapped girls as well as girls' rights to formal education.
>
> (p. 268)

Over time, other politicians and advocates joined the campaign such as British Prime Minister David Cameron, Malala Yousafzai, and U.S. Secretary of State Hillary Clinton. U.S. First Lady Michelle Obama supported the campaign on social media and spoke about the abduction at a White House gathering in May 2014 that promoted girls education (Thompson, 2014, May 22). There were also public demonstrations that took place offline.

Since the abduction in April 2014, many kidnapped girls have been released. In October 2016, 21 girls returned home, and in May 2017, 82 girls were reunited with their families in exchange for five Boko Haram commanders (Associated Press, 2017, May 20). As of summer 2017, many abducted schoolgirls remain missing, but ongoing efforts to locate these girls and bring them home continue. Clearly, the kidnapped schoolgirls experienced emotional resource deprivation through their lack of inclusion, acceptance, and safety at the hands of Boko Haram. In addition, this case of abduction demonstrates how gender discrimination influenced the girls' experiences of emotional resource deprivation.

The Contribution of the Geographic Setting to Child Poverty

The geographic setting of Chibok in northeastern Nigeria had a strong influence on the schoolgirls' experience of poverty through emotional resource deprivation; the abduction took place amidst tensions that were situated at the intersection of geography, religion, and politics. Although Muslims and Christians live throughout the country today, northern Nigeria is largely Islamic while southern Nigeria is largely Christian. Over the last several years, the beliefs of some Muslims in northern Nigeria have clashed with the influences of western culture, especially in regards to education. Boko Haram, an Islamist group based in northeastern Nigeria, has many followers who object to western education. Loimeier (2012) argued that for Boko Haram, western education "has consequently been seen as both a threat and a symbol of the increasing impact of an alien, colonial, Christian, materialist and corrupt process of Westernization" (p. 139). This impact, according to Boko Haram, has affected Islam's influence in Nigeria along with many aspects of culture, including gender norms. As researchers Zenn and Pearson (2014) have pointed out, one of Boko Haram's goals is to implement strict gender roles toward women in order to control women's conduct and make women vulnerable to discrimination and violence. In the militants' view, western education stands in sharp contrast to their perspectives on gender. However, importantly, scholarship (Loimeier, 2012) has suggested that not all Islamist groups in Nigeria necessarily harbor these same gender views; the Yan Izala reform movement, for instance, is an example of one Islamist group's efforts to support "the political and religious mobilization of women" (p. 141).

In light of this context, the geographic setting of the girls' government secondary school in Chibok became a target for Boko Haram to further its agenda. The school's geographic location in a rural area in Borno State, a main base for Boko Haram, made the school vulnerable to an attack. Furthermore, Boko Haram's discriminatory views about gender roles for women made the girls' kidnapping an opportunity for the militant group to impose its beliefs on the girls, the people of Chibok, and northern Nigeria more broadly. No doubt, the education the Nigerian girls received at the secondary school in Chibok was objectionable to Boko Haram as the group aimed to limit the school's influence by invading the school and abducting its students. As a result, the Nigerian schoolgirls encountered emotional resource deprivation through a lack of inclusion, acceptance, and safety due to Boko Haram's violence. The geographic setting of Chibok, coupled with existing socioeconomic disadvantage in northern Nigeria that touched many residents' lives (Egiegba Agbiboa, 2013), had a strong influence on the schoolgirls' kidnapping and their experience of poverty.

Implications and Conclusion

The three cases presented in this chapter illustrate how children in three different contexts—the United States, Ireland, and Nigeria—experienced poverty through material, spiritual, and emotional resource deprivations. This chapter also argued that geographic settings contributed to the experiences of poverty that the children in each location encountered. However, no matter how or where children experience poverty throughout the world, it has important implications for how young people grow and develop, particularly in terms of their development as citizens.

In 1989, the United Nations Convention on the Rights of the Child affirmed children's rights to grow up safely and in good health. Too often, however, these rights are not fully acknowledged and honored, and as a result, many children do not receive the care they need. A lack of adequate care in terms of material, spiritual, and/or emotional resources could have deleterious effects on the lives of these young people and lead these children to be oppressed and marginalized in their lives. This oppression and marginalization could even continue into adulthood and put these young people at a significant disadvantage later in life, likely limiting their engagement as citizens.

To mitigate the ill effects of child poverty in relation to citizenship development, communities must provide young people with the necessary resources, knowledge, and skills to engage as productive and equal members of society. In addition to receiving resources that attend to material, spiritual, and emotional needs, youths must be shown how to identify and challenge inequalities in their communities and how to find solutions to solve problems that touch their (and other citizens') lives. Supportive adults and mentors, therefore, are crucial to constructive citizenship development for these children. These adults and mentors should not only look out for the youths' safety, but also demonstrate engaged and deliberative citizenship themselves. Schools have an important role in achieving this goal. As multicultural education scholars (e.g., Banks et al., 2001; Banks, 2016; Osler & Starkey, 2003) argue, schools are vital in sustaining free and democratic societies that help students form unity among diversity and that promote core values such as equality, justice, and peace. In order for schools to accomplish this work, teachers, in particular, must be adequately prepared to educate youths for active membership in democratic societies (Nieto, 2016). Adults who demonstrate active and engaged citizenship for youths can have lasting positive effects on the lives of young people and help these youths understand how to identify and challenge inequalities that they and other citizens encounter. The knowledge and skills children acquire from their education as young people, therefore, can be a key part in helping these youths develop into engaged citizens who combat injustices in their communities and work to eradicate larger societal and systemic problems, such as child poverty, in all of its forms.

References

Associated Press. (2017). Nigerian schoolgirls kidnapped by Boko Haram rejoin families. *The New York Times*. Retrieved from www.nytimes.com.

Banks, J. A. (2016). Civic education in the age of global migration. In J. A. Banks, M. M. Suárez-Orozco, & M. Ben-Peretz (Eds.), *Global migration, diversity, and civic education* (pp. 29–52). New York: Teachers College Press.

Banks, J. A., Cookson, P., Gay, G., Hawley, W. D., Irvine, J. J., Nieto, S., Schofield, J. W., & Stephan, W. G. (2001). *Diversity within unity: Essential principles for teaching and learning in a multicultural society*. Seattle, WA: University of Washington, Center for Multicultural Education.

Bryan, A. (2009). "Migration nation": Intercultural education and anti-racism as symbolic violence in Celtic Tiger Ireland. In F. Vavrus & L. Bartlett (Eds.), *Critical approaches to comparative education: Vertical case studies from Africa, Europe, the Middle East and the Americas* (pp. 129–145). New York: Palgrave Macmillan.

Central Statistics Office, Ireland (2017). *Census 2016 Summary Results: Part 1*. Cork, Ireland: Central Statistics Office. Retrieved from www.cso.ie/en/media/csoie/news-events/documents/census2016summaryresultspart1/Census2016SummaryPart1.pdf.

Chang, J. (2016, April 27). Nigeria's stolen girls: Inside Boko Haram territory where children are forced to become suicide bombers: Reporters notebook. *ABC News*. Retrieved from abcnews.go.com.

Chiluwa, I., & Ifukor, P. (2015). "War against our children": Stance and evaluation in *#BringBackOurGirls* campaign discourse on Twitter and Facebook. *Discourse & Society 26*(3), 267–296.

Department of Education and Skills (2005). *DEIS (Delivering equality of opportunity in schools): An action plan for educational inclusion*. Retrieved from www.education.ie/en/Publications/Policy-Reports/deis_action_plan_on_educational_inclusion.pdf.

Devine, D. (2011). *Immigration and schooling in the Republic of Ireland: Making a difference?* Manchester, UK: Manchester University Press.

Devine, D., Kenny, M., & Macneela, E. (2008). Naming the "other": Children's construction and experience of racisms in Irish primary schools. *Race, Ethnicity and Education 11*(4), 369–385.

Egiegba Agbiboa, D. (2013). Why Boko Haram exists: The relative deprivation perspective. *African Conflict and Peacebuilding Review 3*(1), 144–157.

Elden, S. (2014). The geopolitics of Boko Haram and Nigeria's "war on terror". *The Geographic Journal 180*(4), 414–425.

Fanning, B. (2002) *Racism and social change in the Republic of Ireland*. Manchester, UK: Manchester University Press.

Gray, K. (2017, April 25). On 3-year anniversary, change is slow for Flint. *Detroit Free Press*. Retrieved from www.freep.com.

Hanna-Attisha, M., LaChance, J., Sadler, R., & Champney Schnepp, A. (2016). Elevated blood lead levels in children associated with the Flint drinking water crisis: A spatial analysis of risk and public health response. *American Journal of Public Health 106*(2), 283–290.

Kennedy, M. (2016, April 20). Lead-laced water in Flint: A step-by-step look at the makings of a crisis. *National Public Radio*. Retrieved from www.npr.org.

Loimeier, R. (2012). Boko Haram: The development of a militant religious movement in Nigeria. *Africa Spectrum 47*(2–3), 137–155.

McClure, D. R. (2016). *"They look at your color": Children of Nigerian immigrants in the Republic of Ireland and their beliefs and expressions of being Irish* (Doctoral dissertation). Retrieved from ProQuest (10138200).

Nieto, S. (2016). Education in a globalized world: Challenges, tensions, possibilities, and implications for teacher education. In J. A. Banks, M. M. Suárez-Orozco, & M. Ben-Peretz (Eds.), *Global migration, diversity, and civic education* (pp. 202–222). New York: Teachers College Press.

Nigeria Chibok Abductions: What We Know (2017, May 8). *BBC News*. Retrieved from www.bbc.com.

Okeowo, A. (2014, April 29). Nigeria's stolen girls. *The New Yorker*. Retrieved from www.newyorker.com.

Osler, A., & Starkey, H. (2003). Learning for cosmopolitan citizenship: Theoretical debates and young people's experiences. *Educational Review 55*(3), 243–254.

Peters, M. A. (2014). "Western education is sinful": Boko Haram and the abduction of Chibok schoolgirls. *Policy Futures in Education 12*(2), 186–190.

Sadler, R. C., & Highsmith, A. R. (2016). Rethinking Tiebout: The contribution of political fragmentation and racial/economic segregation to the Flint water crisis. *Environmental Justice 9*(5), 143–151.

Sieff, K. (2016, April 14). Boko Haram kidnapped 276 girls two years ago. What happened to them? *The Washington Post*. Retrieved from www.washingtonpost.com.

Thompson, K. (2014, May 22). Michelle Obama renews her call to #BringBack OurGirls. *The Washington Post*. Retrieved from www.washingtonpost.com.

UNICEF (2004). *The state of the world's children 2005: Childhood under threat*. Retrieved from www.unicef.org/publications/files/SOWC_2005_(English).pdf.

UNICEF (2007). *Global study on child poverty and disparities 2007–2008 guide*. Retrieved from www.unicef.org/socialpolicy/files/UNICEFGlobalStudyGuide.pdf.

UNICEF & World Bank Group (2016). *Ending extreme poverty: A focus on children*. Retrieved from www.unicef.org/publications/files/Ending_Extreme_Poverty_A_Focus_on_Children_Oct_2016.pdf.

U.S. Department of Commerce, U.S. Census Bureau (2015). *Quick facts: Flint city, Michigan*. Retrieved from www.census.gov/quickfacts/table/PST045215/2629000.

U.S. Department of Commerce, U.S. Census Bureau (2016). *Income and poverty in the United States: 2015*. Retrieved from www.census.gov/content/dam/Census/library/publications/2016/demo/p60-256.pdf.

U.S. Department of Health and Human Services, Centers for Disease Control and Prevention. (2005). *Preventing lead poisoning in young children*. Retrieved from www.cdc.gov/nceh/lead/publications/prevleadpoisoning.pdf.

Watson, I., Phádraig, M., Kennedy, F., & Rock-Huspatel, B. (2007). National identity and anti-immigrant attitudes. In B. Hilliard & M. Phádraig (Eds.),

Changing Ireland in international comparison (pp. 217–242). Dublin, Ireland: The Liffey Press.

White, E. J. (2012). *Modernity, freedom, and the African diaspora: Dublin, New Orleans, Paris.* Bloomington, IN: Indiana University Press.

Zenn, J., & Pearson, E. (2014). Women, gender, and the evolving tactics of Boko Haram. *Journal of Terrorism Research* 5(1), 46–57.

Index

146   *Index*

marketing 57, 58–66
Martin, Bill Jr. 38
Maslow, A. H. 34
Massachusetts 82, 84
material deprivation 130, 131–133, 141
materials 28, 123; *see also* resources
mathematics 14, 20–29;
    Connect4Learning curriculum 124;
    math gap 8; standards 13; Turnaround
    Arts school program 95
Maynard, N. 100
Medicaid 50–51
medical conditions 43–51, 52
medications 44, 45, 47–48, 50
mental health 47–49, 57, 58, 77
mentoring 8, 102
Metcalf, A. 1
Michigan 131–133
Mick, D. G. 59
Midgette, A. 104
Minneapolis 76
minority-owned business services 63–65
mobile devices 5
modeling 40
Morabito, Nancy P. 119–129
motivation 104–105
Mott Haven-Port Morris Land Trust 77
"mouse problem" 1
Moynihan, Daniel Patrick 115
multicultural education 141
multiplication 27
music 95, 96, 112, 116

"A Nation at Risk" (1983) 13, 35
National Center for Children in Poverty
    34, 51–52, 63
National Center for Education Statistics
    (NCES) 96
National Institute of Health (NIH) 17
National Science Teachers Association
    (NSTA) 120, 121
Native Americans 70, 92
navigation 23, 24–25
NCES *see* National Center for Education
    Statistics
NCLB *see* No Child Left Behind
neighborhood violence 7–8, 9
neoconstructivism 20
neoliberalism 71
Ness, Daniel 9–10, 13–32
New Orleans 76
New York City: Brace's philanthropy
    84–85; Community Schools Initiative
    8–9; cost of sports classes 114;

food 2–3, 5; grassroots food justice
    movements 76, 77; House of Refuge
    84; Residential Internship for
    St. John's Educators 36–37
New York Society for the Prevention of
    Cruelty to Children 85
Newcombe, N. S. 20
Next Generation Science Standards
    (NGSS) 120, 121, 123
Nigeria: abducted schoolgirls in 137–141;
    Nigerian immigrants in Ireland
    133–137
NIH *see* National Institute of Health
No Child Left Behind (NCLB) 13, 14,
    35, 96
Noble, K. G. 17
Norman, M. F. 17
NSTA *see* National Science Teachers
    Association
nutrition-related disorders 46–47, 58, 73

Oakland 76
Obama, Barack 34, 35, 103–104, 109, 139
Obama, Michelle 109
obesity 46–47, 51–52, 62, 73, 109, 113, 117
observation 123, 125–127
Ohanian, S. 112
Okely, A. D. 113
Okeowo, A. 139
Oliver, K. M. 103
OneUnited Bank 64
oppression 70, 141
oral health 49, 51–52; *see also* dental care
Orphan Train movement 85
Orwellian language 13, 29
Ozanne, J. L. 59

parens patriae 86, 89
parenting 113
Parsad, B. 96
Pearson, E. 140
Pechmann, C. 59
Peppler, K. 100
Peters, M. A. 139
Pettigrew, S. 59
Phádraig, M. 136
Philadelphia 76, 90
physical activity 109–118
Piaget, J. 14, 20
Pinar, W. F. 15
PIRLS *see* Progress in International
    Reading Literacy Study
PISA *see* Programme for International
    Student Assessment